Chambers

£3

GW01072010

job applications

Chambers

CHAMBERS

An imprint of Chambers Harrap Publishers Ltd

7 Hopetoun Crescent

Edinburgh EH7 4AY

First published by Chambers Harrap Publishers Ltd 2006

© Chambers Harrap Publishers Ltd 2006

A CIP catalogue record for this book is available from the British Library.

ISBN-13: 978 0550 10243 0

ISBN-10: 0550 10243 4

Designed and typeset by Chambers Harrap Publishers Ltd, Edinburgh

Printed and bound in Spain by GraphyCems

CONTRIBUTORS

Text
Gary Dexter

Editors
Sheila Ferguson
Mary O'Neill

Publishing Manager
Patrick White

Prepress Controller
Isla MacLean

Prepress Manager
Clair Simpson

CONTENTS

Introduction

Applying for a job is a bit like speed dating.

Imagine the following scene: twenty single people, all looking for romance, are packed together in a small room. In turn, they each get a chance to speak to an attractive potential partner in the next room. Each turn lasts only two minutes. In that brief time, every one of the hopefuls must make enough of an impact to outdistance their competitors in order to get a date.

As you have probably guessed, the twenty single people are the job-seekers, and their possible future companion is the employer. The two-minute speed date is the CV/application stage, and the real date is the interview. If the candidate passes both stages they have found a partner, or, in employment terms, they have got the job.

Potential employers are generally in the business of selecting from a number of candidates. This involves rejecting the many and considering the few. They are looking for a reason to put candidates' details in the shredder. They only have a moment to glance at a life in all its richness. If there is anything wrong with the applicant, even something minor, it could spell rejection.

Among the things that employers have a bias against are sickness, pusillanimity, poor hygiene, sloppiness, any negative aspects of ageing, lack of qualifications, and lack of interest.

The key to winning them over is to examine what you have to offer and then present your assets and your good qualities in the most appealing way possible. This is, surprisingly, as much about leaving things out as putting things in. When you have only a short time to impress someone you should omit potentially negative points, for example periods of unemployment or date of birth.

If it reflects badly on you, do not mention it unless you have to. You must, of course, be ready to field awkward questions and explain gaps, but that's for the interview. You can finesse the bad news then, at your convenience.

So, to sum up, you are probably going to be facing competition, and you will have to go one better than your competitors to succeed. To do this you will need to make an immediate good impression at the CV/application stage and follow that up with a confident and appealing presentation at interview.

This may sound rather daunting. Do not worry. This book will show you exactly how to do it.

Part One

CVs

CVs: the basics

Successful CVs may come in various formats. However, essentially they contain only two main types of information: skills and achievements. Some CVs will focus more on skills while others will concentrate more on achievements.

Here is a brief overview of each:

SKILLS-BASED CVs

A CV that focuses mainly on skills will seek to describe a person's capabilities rather than listing jobs or achievements. It will use its various sections to foreground a person's professional profile; the areas in which they have had an impact at work; their technical proficiencies and strengths. It may include a mission statement or career objective. The candidate's employment history need not be given in any more than skeletal detail; for example, it could appear in a section headed 'Career highlights' or 'Selected accomplishments'.

A skills-based CV is useful for people who have had a break from employment and do not wish to draw immediate attention to the fact; for example, women returning to work after having or raising children, recent graduates who do not have much or any employment history, or people changing careers.

Skills-based CVs are described in more detail on page 8.

ACHIEVEMENT-BASED CVs

An achievement-based CV will focus on things actually done – that is, it will be linked to real places, jobs and events. 'Achievement' is a key word here. It does not necessarily mean what you were responsible for in any particular job, since it is quite possible to have responsibility without achievement.

An achievement-based CV will usually have a detailed reverse-chronological employment history, linking the candidate's work experience to their achievements. It will illustrate the benefits that past achievements brought to previous employers and quantify those benefits in real numbers. It may also give a more detailed educational history.

Achievement-based CVs are described in more detail on page 11.

Although you will be able to ring the changes on these two basic ingredients in a number of ways, it is comforting to remember that CVs are fundamentally concerned with these two aspects: skills and achievements.

Building blocks

CVs are built in blocks of text. This helps to differentiate the various types of information so that the page does not present a solid mass of print. A block structure makes a CV easy on the eye and easy on the brain of the reader. It enables the reader to find the information they want quickly – or, to be more precise, it enables the reader to locate quickly the information that the CV-writer wants them to.

What follows are the most common building blocks.

Career profile

A career profile (also known as a career statement, or professional profile, or key facts section) is a brief statement of the type of person you are, your experience, education and training and personal qualities. It nearly always precedes the main body of the CV, that is it sits at the top, and puts the most positive spin possible on the facts. Here's an example:

> *Profile: A well-organized, highly motivated individual with a Master's degree in Business Administration and seven years' experience in equipment sales. Ranked as a top company earner, with demonstrated ability to build customer rapport and clinch sales.*

For more examples of career profiles, and the way to write them, see page 21.

Career objective

A career objective (also known as a career goal, or objective, or professional objective) is an opportunity to say, in a few words, what you are looking for at this point in your career.

It is not absolutely essential to have a career objective and it may be superfluous if applying for an advertised position, but if it hits the desk of an employer looking for someone like you, it could work wonders. Here's an example:

> *Objective: A position as a telemarketing specialist that will make productive use of proven abilities in team-building and creative problem-solving.*

For more examples of career objectives and the way to write them see page 26.

CVS: THE BASICS

Personal details

This is probably the section that most people could do with pruning. It should be purely functional, giving very basic information, and not a space-waster.

For more on personal details see page 28.

Key skills

This section, perhaps entitled 'Skills summary', 'Demonstrated strengths', 'Areas of impact', 'Key strengths' or any one of a number of other formulations, has one purpose: to give, in concrete terms, a list of the CV-writer's major abilities. It will form an important part of a skills-based CV when, for whatever reason, work experience is not the area that is emphasized.

For more details on key skills see page 30.

Work experience

Work experience will, of course, have more prominence in an achievement-based CV. Like other sections, it should demonstrate that you are potentially of value to an employer. The section need not be exhaustive, and could be headed 'Selected achievements' or 'Employment highlights'. Where it exists it should be linked to real actions and achievements that will make the reader recognize that this is a useful person, rather than simply stating a series of job titles.

For more details on work experience see page 35.

Educational qualifications

Like 'Personal details', this is an area that could benefit from being reduced. It is not necessary to give details of every exam you have ever passed. Higher qualifications automatically imply lower ones.

For more details on educational qualifications see page 41.

Interests

Interests (avoid the word 'hobbies') are an optional part of a CV, and because of the importance of brevity they can be left out altogether. They are there, if at all, to give the reader an impression of what a valuable employee you would be, and as such they should be selected with care.

For more details on interests see page 43.

References and endorsements

The current style is not to give references at all, but to put simply 'References available on request'. Endorsements, on the other hand, are actual quotes from people who know you, and these can appear right in the middle of the CV itself. This is a very bold strategy but can be effective.

A discussion of references and endorsements, including the arguments for and against, is given on page 45.

These are the basic elements of a CV. If you follow the advice above and cut some aspects of it, you may be left with a document that fits on a page. This is good. The one-page CV is now preferred by the majority of employers. One page is easy to file, easy to scan into a database and easy to read. And there is plenty of room on one page to say exactly what needs to be said and to outdistance the competition.

Skills-based CVs

Let's start this section by looking at a typical skills-based CV. The one on page 9 is by a technical draughtsman who now wants to switch and do something different, in this case, to teach Design Technology at secondary school level. He has taken the first step by completing a teacher-training course (PGCE).

Obviously he can't focus too heavily on his achievements in the field of technical draughtsmanship. He needs to focus on his skills. That is, he needs to emphasize the sort of person he is and what he can offer as a person. That means trying to extract from his experiences the qualities that will make him attractive as a potential teacher.

Here are some things to notice about Bill's CV:

1. It fits on one A4 page. This signals that the applicant is aware of the benefits of concision, and helps the reader scan the information quickly to find what they want.

2. It is tailored to a particular position: this is a sensible approach. If Bill changes his mind and decides to specialize in something else, he will have to rewrite it. Job-hunters must be prepared to have more than one CV.

3. The CV demonstrates that he can offer something of value to the employer despite the absence of any paid teaching experience. By focusing on his teaching placement and downplaying his career as a draughtsman, Bill is promoting his enthusiasm, pride and motivation with regard to his new career.

Bill Righton
62 Oyster Rd, Bristol BS5 5FT
(01234) 56789
b.righton@anyserver.com

Profile
Professional and qualified teacher with experience in ICT/CADCAM and a high level of
self-motivation, energy and enthusiasm, as well as good organization and interpersonal
skills.

Teaching experience
- Placement at Hoxton Middle School, from September 2004-July 2005 while on
  PGCE course, teaching Design Technology at key stages 3 and 4.
- Worked in the classroom with CAD/CAM facilities including CAMM1, CAMM2,
  Denford CNC Miller, CNC Router and CNC Lathe. Experienced with software
  including Pro-Desk, 2D Designer, Crocodile Technology and PCB Wizard.
- Supported children in a number of courses including Built Environment, Motor
  Vehicle Maintenance (in collaboration with Burnell College), Alternative Technology
  and Industrial Design.
- Gained extensive experience in lesson planning using structured teaching
  programmes and performance tracking.
- Motivated and encouraged children to achieve highest GCSE marks in school's history.
- Developed new programmes for children with learning disabilities using interactive ICT.
- Personal achievements on the course included: enhanced ability to communicate
  effectively and appropriately with children, parents and colleagues; implementation
  of health and safety regulations; ability to work under pressure to achieve
  deadlines in a school environment.
- Accompanied children on school trip abroad.

Other professional competencies
- Background in technical drawing and industrial design at a professional level.
- Disciplined and motivated in work habits.
- Flexible self-starter who is able to respond to a variety of technical and interpersonal
  challenges.
- Proficient in a wide range of computer applications beyond technical drawing and
  design, among them Windows XP Professional, Microsoft Office, ClarisWorks, Word
  processing, Spreadsheets and the Internet.

Career history

Senior Draughtsman, British Oxygen	2001–2004
Senior Draughtsman, Siemens Electronics	1995–2001
Freelance Consultant, Baghdad Oil and Gas	1986–95
Freelance Draughtsman, Algol International	1983–86
Piping Designer, Larkman Inc.	1975–83

Educational
Bachelor of Science, London University
BTEC Diploma

Personal
D.o.b.: 25.10.54
Status: Married, two children

REFERENCES AND OTHER SUPPORTING DATA AVAILABLE ON REQUEST

4. Although Bill's teaching experience was essentially in a supportive role, the CV does not mention the word 'support' or 'supported'; instead it concentrates on his active input into the new situation.

5. The CV is short on educational history, personal details, outside interests and career history, precisely because it is long on teaching skills.

6. It doesn't mention pay or salary; in the oil industry Bill earned a lot more than he will as a teacher, and there is no point in making invidious comparisons.

7. The date of the degree is not given. Of course, such information is available on request, but since it was done at least a quarter of a century ago, mention of it would only emphasize Bill's age and perhaps rule him out for interview.

8. The CV will provide an interviewer with cues for structuring the interview, should Bill get one. More importantly, they are the cues that Bill has determined.

In summary, skills-based CVs emphasize human potential. They sell a person's qualities rather than their achievements. When you are happier to talk about your achievements you need a different approach.

Achievement-based CVs

Achievement-based CVs are what most people envisage when thinking about a CV – the traditional 'tombstone' approach with a name and some dates. But achievement-based CVs do not have to induce the melancholy of a graveyard. Achievement-based CVs are an opportunity for you to make yourself look exciting. Nor should they be thought of as a black-and-white alternative to skills-based CVs; the two types interpenetrate one another. It is a question of emphasis.

Let's start with the CV on the following page by way of example. This one is from a highly successful marketing manager.

Here are some things you might notice about this CV:

1. It is an achievement-based (ie a work-experience-based) CV, but it still has a feeling of excitement and dynamism. That is important. The person reading it may already have seen 139 CVs that morning.

2. Again, it is different in layout from the preceding CV. It has only three main sections: Summary (ie Profile), Career highlights and Professional experience. Do not be afraid to experiment with layout. There is an infinite number of ways of ringing the changes on the basic information.

3. The Profile section, here called 'Summary', is lengthy and detailed. This is the hard sell at the top of the CV. It gives an impression of a very experienced person with a lot to be proud of and who is not afraid, in a measured and dignified way, to tell you about it.

Elaine Anderson

56 The Street, Manchester M60 2LR · 01234 56789 · e.anderson@anyserver.co.uk

Summary

A talented, technically-proficient marketing manager with 12+ years' experience. Self-motivated and enthusiastic, with excellent interpersonal skills at all company levels. Demonstrated achievements include strong analytical skills, award-winning sales presentations and successful new product introductions. Excels in meeting targets.

Career highlights

- Implemented corporate marketing plan in Argentina, working closely with the parent company's product and marketing teams.
- Managed over 80 programmes annually from 1998–2004.
- Achievement award from the Institute of Marketing Managers 2002 for Creative Marketing following successful introduction of a new range of hygiene products.
- Consistently met deadlines with a success rate of 91% (career average).
- Increased awareness of brand in Belize by 300% through development of creative programmes, brand awareness campaigns and promotions.
- Developed the innovative 'Tools and collateral pack' which won the 1998 award for Marketing Solutions from *Merchandising Monthly* magazine, designed to help resellers to create an event strategy to effectively sell the company's advertising products.
- Turned around ailing branch offices.
- Targeted poorly-performing accounts, increasing sales figures by 70% overall.
- Managed marketing merger of a consortium of companies resulting in synergies that increased feature activity from 40% to 80%.
- Monitored consumer, industry and competitive behaviour in Venezuela and provided local market expertise to the UK team.
- Developed and implemented ongoing retention programmes and managed advertiser and publisher communications, resulting in a 30% upturn in sales.
- Managed the company's country marketing budget of over £2 million for Argentina in 1998–2001.

Professional experience

Alcock International Footwear Ltd
Sales and Marketing Manager   1995 to present
Devised marketing plans and direct marketing activity for the company's products or services, particularly in Latin America. Identified target markets, developed and monitored new campaigns, created new promotions and presentations, managed budgets and wrote proposals. Evaluated trade shows and industry events to gauge suitability for the company's products and/or sponsorship.

Avalon Foods Ltd
Marketing Manager   1992–1995
Created and monitored marketing campaigns. Worked closely with team members
and other departments to implement local marketing programmes with a
combination of marketing tactics including affiliate marketing, events and seminars,
online advertising and direct marketing. Worked to grow key retail accounts and
foster distributor relationships.

Education and professional affiliations

BSc in Business Administration, 1993
MBA, University of East Anglia, 1994
Chartered Institute of Marketing Diploma, 1994
Senior Member of the Institute of Direct Marketing and the Institute of Sales and
Marketing Management

Computer skills

Windows XP Professional, Visual Basic, Excel, FCS-EPS software

Personal

D.o.b. 30.6.75
Married, two children

References available on request

4. The work experience section is split into two: Career highlights, conveying a concise sense of achievement to the reader; and Professional experience, which gives details of where and when. It is possible to merge the two and still keep the same impression of dynamism and achievement, but by presenting it this way the recruiter is faced immediately with the collected achievements of the applicant.

5. The achievements are quantified in number or percentage terms. Statistics are of course contentious, but you can contend them to your heart's content once you have got the interview.

6. There is a blizzard of words ending in '-ed', chosen for their power. These are all action words, giving the strong impression of achievement, and perhaps more to the point, finality. If something is expressed in the past it shows, above all, that it has

been done. The present continuous (implementing, analyzing, managing, etc), quite common in CVs, is not so powerful, since it leaves the unconscious impression that the activity is still in progress and thus has an unknown final outcome.

7. As with all CVs, this document is going to form an important point of reference in any interview. The interviewee has a head start – she can anticipate with reasonable certainty what the questions might be, and, more importantly, they allow her an opportunity to talk about her achievements.

8. She doesn't say why she is leaving her job, despite being so successful. She may be relocating; perhaps she wants promotion; perhaps she would like more money; perhaps she was dismissed. Whatever the reason, none of these feature on her CV. None of them reflect well on her loyalties to or relationship with her old employer, and her new employer will be understandably sensitive about this. If they decide they want her, they are going to want to keep her, since recruiting, for them, is a tiresome and expensive business. Discussions about reasons for leaving are thus better kept for the interview – if they have to be mentioned at all.

In summary, achievement-based CVs emphasize things that have demonstrably been done. They sell a person's potential for the future by reference to their achievements in the past. They are useful for people with an established track record who are happy to boast about it. At their best they should be exciting and impressive, and provide an opportunity to create something eye-catching and different.

Layout

How you lay out your CV gives you one of your best chances to create something individual, and an opportunity to make an impression.

In the examples given so far we have seen that it is possible to take the basic ingredients of a CV – profile, work experience, key skills, personal details, educational qualifications, and so on – and shape them to fit the needs of a particular CV-writer. What's more, you can call any section whatever you like. 'Key skills' can be 'strengths' or 'key capabilities' or 'areas of proven ability'. As long as the really essential information is there, you have the chance to create something that looks really distinctive.

Order of sections

There are no hard and fast rules on what order to put your sections in. One effective strategy, however, is to look at the CV through the eyes of the employer. He or she probably doesn't want to see your marital status, interests, or education at the top of the CV. He or she wants to know immediately what value you can bring to the company. Bearing that in mind, the following is a good order:

1. Contact details
2. Profile
3. Career objective
4. Key skills
5. Work experience
6. Education
7. Interests
8. Personal details
9. References

This gives your contact information the most prominence to encourage quick action. It then works through your career with reasonable attention to what you have to offer. If, however, you are a recent graduate, then your educational details may come higher up the list.

Title of sections

But of course these sections could be labelled completely differently, as follows:

1. Contact (usually no title)
2. Summary
3. Objective
4. Areas of expertise
5. Achievements
6. Qualifications
7. Community involvement
8. Personal
9. Referees

Since some of these sections are optional, one might end up with the following:

1. Contact
2. Summary
3. Areas of expertise
4. Achievements
5. Qualifications
6. Personal

Within limits, your choices are pretty wide. Other possible section headings include the following:

Profile	professional profile; career profile; summary
Objective	career objective; professional objective
Key skills	technical expertise; skills summary; strengths; areas of knowledge and ability; technical profile; areas of knowledge; areas of expertise; areas of effectiveness; areas of strength
Work experience	career highlights and achievements; significant accomplishments; achievements; career chronology; experience highlights; career highlights; experience; experience and selected accomplishments; recent achievements/earlier achievements; employment history; performance highlights; recent projects; professional experience
Education and training	additional training; professional qualifications; educational awards; summary of qualifications; affiliations; qualifications summary; education; professional affiliations; education and personal
Interests	community involvement; out-of-work activities/interests/pursuits
References	referees; endorsements; selected references

Page layout

So far we have talked about laying out your CV according to order and title of sections, but what about appearance on the page? The following diagrams show a variety of one-page CV designs with some points to note.

LAYOUT

Figure 1: This layout has got a lot going for it. It is not cluttered, so the recruiter is not going to feel that the information has been recklessly crammed onto the page. However, it has a drawback: there is too little space at the bottom margin. If you think of the way exhibition posters are presented, you will often notice that there is a white space at the bottom. This gives the poster a sense of balance.

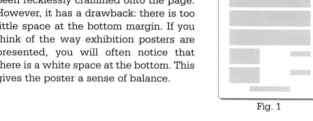

Fig. 1

Figure 2: This example is the same but has the bottom margin wider than the top. You can see that it appears better balanced.

Fig. 2

Figure 3: This example suffers from excessive heaviness. The blocks of text, doubtless impressive if one were to read them, are ponderous, and the layout is unimaginative. Anyone with a pile of CVs in front of them might quail slightly at this and be reluctant to read it all.

Fig. 3

Fig. 4

Figure 4: This example is, to an extent, the opposite; the layout is broken up into many bite-sized chunks. There is nothing necessarily wrong with this, but its success would probably depend on which information went in which box. If the small boxes were to contain dates, this would be best avoided. Dates should go on the right-hand side, not the left, on the principle that the eye scans from left to right, and dates are of secondary importance to the skill or achievement itself.

Fig. 5

Figure 5: This example gets away from the blocky style of the preceding two examples and uses centralization to create a more attractive layout. In this case, however, there is too little information on the page; the layout looks like a restaurant menu. The reader would be forgiven for thinking that the CV-writer doesn't have much to say. If you do not have enough material to fill out your CV, include an expanded skills section or use the prominent placing of endorsements to make an impression.

Fig. 6

Figure 6: This example also uses centralization but gives a much better balance. It also makes use of a couple of other strategies. An early section (possibly a skills section or a profile) is enclosed in a box for greater emphasis, nicely breaking up the page. Further down, a final section is split into three groups, possibly of bulleted points, which are then centred on the page.

Figure 7: Here's an example of all left-ranged text which compares with figure 5. Possibly because of a dearth of information, there is too much white space at the right. The all-left-ranged approach also speaks of a certain lack of imagination.

Fig. 7

Figure 8: Here we have another CV using both left-ranged text and centralization, plus the use of columns. One aspect of this that may not immediately be noticeable is that is has alternating margins: if you look at the margins for the second, fourth and sixth rows, they line up; so do the margins for the third and fifth. This gives an attractive sense of balance.

Fig. 8

These are just some examples of layout. You may wish to create your own.

A career profile (also known as a career statement, or professional profile, or key facts section) is a way of summarizing your value to the recruiter. Between one and three sentences is enough – it should not be too long, since the information it contains will, by its nature, be repeated in the main body of the CV. Its content should give the impression that you have a background of demonstrable achievement and the skills to make a valuable contribution to a future employer. It will usually, if not always, precede the main CV, since part of its job is to make a favourable first impression. It should therefore be concise, pertinent and attention-grabbing.

As well as helping the employer make a decision on what you have to offer, it also helps you, in two main ways:

- It helps you decide generally on how you want to present yourself and what you want out of your career, which can be useful later on.
- It helps you decide what to put in the body of the CV and what to leave out of it, since the CV should support the career profile.

Profile brainstorm
So how do you arrive at a profile?

Let's look back at the starting point of CV-writing. There are only two useful types of information, skills and achievements. Now take each of those two types and break them down:

CAREER PROFILE

Skills	Education
	Attributes
	Knowledge
Achievements	Experience
	Success
	Unique selling point (USP)

Take a piece of paper and a pen and write down the main things you associate with each of those six areas. For example, a mental health nurse might write:

Education:	degree, RGN
Attributes:	passionate about high standards, good people-person
Knowledge:	capable of working flexibly with service users who have complex needs
Experience:	12 years' experience
Success:	organizational skills tested in setting up new programmes
USP:	specializing in detoxification from sub-stance misuse

He or she needn't put all of this in; it is a guide. Prioritized and put together this might read something like:

> *Mental health nurse with degree, RGN qualification and 12 years' experience, capable of working flexibly with service users who have complex needs, both in the community and in sheltered accommodation. Passionate about, and committed to delivering, the highest standards of care, with proven organizational skills.*

Note that this is expressed in the third person. It sounds more objective, despite the fact that the material in it is self-authored and unequivocally glowing. In the third person it seems less arrogant.

Specific title or no title?

The profile section can, as mentioned above, have a number of different titles. One strategy is to head it, for example, 'Manager profile' to make it clear from the start that the CV is aiming specifically for that post. A further strategy is to have your profile unheaded and just to lead off with your main areas of strength immediately after your address:

James Goldburn
123 Covert Close
Peterborough PT1 2ED
01234 56789

International espionage · Weapons handling · Assassination · Casino work

Example profiles

Here are some other examples of career profiles:

Graduate in Hotel Management with 3 years' experience of F & B departments. Excellent spoken and written English and good administrative ability. Self-motivated, and able to motivate others, with excellent communication and interpersonal skills.

An analyst with five years' experience within the pharmaceutical industry, specializing in analytical (HPLC) method development, validation and troubleshooting. An active planner and manager who is adept at mentoring and motivating less experienced staff.

Café Bar Manager able to provide an excellent catering service and with a track record of boosting profitability. Flexible in working approach, with relevant food and hygiene qualifications equivalent to NVQ level 2.

Business and Performance Manager with three years' experience working with key Criminal Justice Service agencies. Excellent communication and organizational skills and the capability to resolve complex problems. A confident and creative team leader.

Young and energetic book-keeper, experienced in all aspects of MS Office software and with a sound knowledge of book-keeping procedures within a small business environment, including computerized accounts packages and the preparation of management accounts. A confident, self-motivated individual with the ability to work in a changing environment.

Dynamic Field Service Engineer with high degree of customer focus and excellent service skills. Demonstrable ability through 6 years' experience of working in a fast-paced industry. A skilled communicator with a 'can-do' attitude.

Sales executive with MBA and a high degree of market awareness on narrow and widebody aircraft for the European, Middle East and African regions. Target-orientated and able to bring contacts and relationships to foster future success. A self-starter with strong customer focus and the ability to initiate, develop and close opportunities.

Highly qualified Landscape Architect with quality imaginative design and master-planning skills and ten years' experience in both the private and public sector. Reliable, conscientious and a confident communicator.

German-speaking Senior Recruitment Manager with 15 years' experience in HR. An innovator adept at finding the right talent and supervising the related administrative work flow, with a strong commitment to building a winning team.

Store manager with strong motivation and high levels of energy, committed to developing teamwork, improving store performance and motivating staff. Excellent communication skills combine with an ability to deal with pressurized situations in a fast-paced, high-volume environment.

All of these show the impact a concise and powerful profile can create.

Career objective

Career objectives are not absolutely necessary. They will probably be of use in the following situations:

- When you wish to demonstrate that you are 'just right' for a post.
- When you wish to emphasize the trend of your career path.
- When you wish to project that your career has 'direction' when in fact you are at the beginning of your career or have changed careers.

They are probably not necessary when:

- You are applying for an advertised post.
- You do not wish to limit yourself in the current application.
- Your objectives are liable to change over the course of time – perhaps months or years – that the CV will be on file.

Example objectives

When thinking about writing an objective, you need to think beyond what you actually want for your career. This may sound paradoxical, but a successful career objective is less about you and more about your employer, the person who is reading the CV. In other words, you need to show you will be a valuable employee: that you are well worth taking on.

With this in mind, here are some examples of career objectives (or career goals, or professional goals):

A post as a senior sales co-ordinator that will provide an opportunity to demonstrate proven communication and organizational skills.

A management position that will allow full use of bilingual and interpersonal skills and draw on experience of European negotiations.

A position as a telemarketing specialist that will make productive use of proven abilities in team-building and creative problem-solving.

A senior position as an analytical chemist in the textiles industry that will demonstrate understanding and expertise in project development and quality control.

A challenging role as a Financial Manager in the food industry that will build on a career as a top company earner.

Like career profiles, the objectives or goals come at the beginning of your CV and act as a structuring device for what is to follow. They may be used in conjunction with a profile or instead of one; it is your choice.

Personal details

Personal details are different from contact details. Contact details are extremely important, and should go at the head of the CV, as follows:

John Smith-Brown
14 Colchester Avenue
Salford
SL2 3RT
01234 56789
j.smithbrown@anyserver.com

Personal details, by contrast, can safely be left to the end. Some of the things that can be included are:

- date of birth
- marital status
- family
- driving licence
- willingness to relocate

Leave it out?

Date of birth can be a tricky issue. If you leave it out, some employers might assume you are getting on in years and discriminate against you. If you put it in, you might be rejected for the same reason, or because you are too young. The best approach is probably to include it as it is likely to be evident from your employment or education dates.

Marital status is another poser. It is certainly not legally required to declare it. If you are married, declaring it can give an impression of solidity and normality, and may be to your advantage. On the other hand, declaring you are married might imply children in some people's minds, and children are not always welcomed by employers.

Neither are you required to mention children. Some employers want their staff to be flexible, and may perhaps view children as an impediment to a relocation. On the other hand, there is the solidity/normality factor. It is another judgement call, but probably coming down on the negative side.

A full clean driving licence is worth mentioning, as is willingness to relocate or travel, where relevant.

Key skills

CVs and advertisements have a lot in common. Both work best if they are brief, eye-catching and offer something irresistible. Advertisements offer benefits: how you can accelerate faster, keep your toilet cleaner, look more attractive. Your CV should do the same – offer benefits. The skills section provides a way to do it.

Skills sections emphasize human potential. They foreground a person's accumulated capabilities. They will obviously feature prominently in skills-based CVs, which, as we have already noted, are useful for:

- career-changers
- those just starting work
- those returning to work after an absence
- people with a long working career who do not wish to emphasize their age, only their capabilities

However, they may also feature in achievement-based CVs where a little extra impact or salesmanship is called for. They will usually be placed around the beginning to the middle of the CV, after the career profile and before the work experience section.

Skills brainstorm

So how do you go about constructing a skills section?

A good way to start is to ask yourself the following questions:

- What tasks do I actually perform in my job every day?

- What active verbs could I pin to those tasks?
  That is, what do I plan, select, carry out, schedule, set up, maintain, supervise, change, construct, manage, handle, administrate, troubleshoot, adapt to, respond to, develop, serve, intervene in, introduce, analyze, decide?

- What personal attributes do I have?
  Am I honest, responsible, enterprising, logical, reliable, dedicated, confident, creative, efficient, competitive, focused, hardworking, active, highly motivated, calm under pressure, highly trained, proficient, organized?

- What interpersonal attributes do I have?
  Am I an effective team player? Do I communicate well? At what levels do I communicate – to staff, management, shop floor? Can I motivate others? Can I negotiate effectively? Am I a good leader? A good manager?

- What are my technical abilities? My specialist training? My computer skills?

You may feel that many of the positive qualities you have come up with by asking yourself those questions are surprising. You are very talented. Of course, you need to be careful not to simply pepper your CV with positive words at random. You will need to be able to support these words at interview. And as with everything on your CV, you must be truthful. It will help if you choose such qualities carefully to fit the overall thrust of your CV (see your career objective for reference). If all or most of these qualities can be backed up and echoed in your work experience section too, so much the better.

Let's have a look at a skills section (here called 'Areas of strength') in context in a CV. This one is from an 18-year-old who left school at 16 with few qualifications and has worked until now mostly in low-level sales positions. She is now applying to get on an accountancy training course which has limited places, so the stakes are high. She will have to fill out an application form to get on the course but there is room for her to submit a CV too. To her this may seem an additional burden, but the hours she spends on it could prove the most valuable.

She cannot stress her experience, mainly because she is young and she has not got much. This is not necessarily a disadvantage. Recruiters and academic staff obviously do not expect young people to be as experienced as older people. However, in a climate in which there will be plenty of applicants competing for the place, the holder of the CV must make herself stand out from the crowd and get an interview. The CV must jolt them into thinking that this young woman deserves a chance to be taken seriously.

Helen's CV is shown on the following page and here are some things to notice about the skills section in it:

1. In the absence of much work experience she uses the 'Areas of strength' section to say as much as possible about her character and personal skills.

2. The positives are spread thickly, but the tone is still cool and professional, not gushing or unrealistic.

3. The skills section and the endorsements section both mention ability to learn, and the CV is an application to go on a course of study. It has been carefully constructed to do a particular job. This is an example of how relevant skills can be pulled from almost any background: if she had wanted to be an art therapist, the keywords would be 'creative', 'imaginative' 'sympathetic', 'interpersonal', and could conceivably be drawn from the same actual life/work experience.

4. It is well-organized and concise – not unimportant qualities for an accountant.

Helen Wilson
12 The Street
Norwich NR3 2RT
Tel 01604 567483
e-mail h.wilson@anyserver.co.uk

OBJECTIVE
Enrolment on an accountancy training course to further a career in banking and the financial services sector.

AREAS OF STRENGTH
- Excellent numerical competence
- Decisive, motivated individual who is quick to learn and determined to succeed
- Computer literate with good word-processing skills
- Good communicator
- Highly trustworthy
- Reputation for reliability

ENDORSEMENTS
Shop manager
'Helen would be in the top ten percent of the many sales people I have trained, for her quick intelligence and immediate grasp of what the situation demanded … she was always friendly and attentive … I would thoroughly recommend her to you as a trainee.'

Maths teacher
'A resourceful young woman who often took the lead in class and was pleasant and polite … her mathematical ability was above average and she would, I am sure, flourish in an environment that allowed it to develop.'

WORK EXPERIENCE
Sales, Brookings Convenience Stores, 2003–present
- Handling of money, credit and debit cards, Chip and PIN transactions
- Training and supervision of new members of staff
- Good record of customer service

TECHNICAL SKILLS
MS Office including Word and Excel; familiarity with Internet; excellent typing at 45 wpm

EDUCATION
Boxton City College, 5 GCSEs, 3 at 'A' grade

PERSONAL
D.o.b. 2.2.88

KEY SKILLS

In summary, then, the skills section is one more chance to make an impact. It emphasizes capability over experience, and is particularly useful for certain types of job-seekers. If you can tailor it to a particular position it will be at its most cogent.

Work experience

The work experience section is where you put your achievements. You can do this in one of two ways:

- You can list your achievements in isolation – that is, without mention of a who, a where and a when – and then relegate the names and dates to the bottom of the CV in a more abbreviated fashion.
- You can tie your achievements to a who, a where and a when.

Either is an acceptable strategy. It is a question of personal taste. The first strategy is more up-front in that it gives a blitz of achievement to startle and impress the reader (see the CV on page 12). The second is more measured but perhaps more traditional and authoritative (see the CV on page 39).

Work experience brainstorm

To start building your work experience section, the best way is to prepare a rough draft. Go over your past and present jobs and remind yourself of all the most basic details. That is:

- when you joined
- how long you were there
- what your job title was at the beginning, and whether it changed
- what your responsibilities were

You won't necessarily include all these details on the CV. For instance, you might want to present the dates you were there by only using the year dates, which might be more advantageous to you if you had a prolonged spell of unemployment. But you still need to know the month dates, perhaps even the calendar dates. It is worth making the effort to remember, because at the interview you are not just going to be asked to recapitulate your CV; you are going to be asked to analyze it, to pick it apart, to elaborate on it. You must be able to put flesh on the bones or you are more liable to give a poor performance at interview. This underlines the importance of truthfulness. Even if the details you give are carefully selected, they must still be accurate, or you might trip yourself up further down the line.

Now you have the basic details you need to sell yourself. Your skills have already been covered. This time you need to give figures, to demonstrate value.

Which achievements should you choose, and how should you present them? To ascertain this, try asking yourself the following questions:

- In each job you did, what was your most significant achievement?
- What was the value of this to your employer?
- How much money did it save or generate?
- How was performance improved?
- How much time did it save (time is money)?
- What was your second most significant achievement in each job?
- What was your third?

Now try putting the basic details together with the achievement details. You might arrive at something like this:

Alexandra School of English, Manningtree   1998–2001

Director of English Language Teaching Programmes

Achievements:

- *Increased student levels by 50%, generating an extra £120,000 in revenue.*
- *Motivated staff to see themselves as 'trainers' rather than teachers, resulting in positive outcomes in staff-student relationships.*
- *Evaluated IT needs, installed eight new workstations and transformed the school's IT capabilities.*

As you can see, this featured a bulleted section, headed 'Achievements'. It could equally well have been written out as a paragraph:

Alexandra School of English, Manningtree   1998–2001

Director of English Language Teaching Programmes

Increased student levels by 50%, generating an extra £120,000 in revenue. Motivated staff to see themselves as 'trainers' rather than teachers, resulting in positive outcomes in staff-student relationships. Evaluated IT needs and transformed the school's IT capabilities.

Once again, the choice is yours.

Here are some things the above example didn't include:

- The name of an actual person who employed you, ie a boss. Just the company name is fine.
- A detailed company address. Just the town or city is fine.
- A salary.
- A reason for leaving the job.

Instead it focused on things more likely to interest the employer, and less likely to act as a distraction or diminish the value of the applicant.

It also acted as a jumping-off point for interview questions. Interviewers whose curiosity is stimulated will want to ask questions, and when you have the answers ready, they'll feel they have done their job too. So everyone gains.

Let's look at a work experience section in context in a CV. It is from a travel agent looking for promotion. After an early false start as a sales assistant in a stationer's shop and some other part-time jobs, his whole career has been in the travel industry, so he has a settled base to build on. He doesn't want to look settled, though. He wants to look dynamic, ambitious and indispensable.

Some things to notice about the work experience section in the following CV are:

1. The 'Professional experience' section is organized in reverse chronological order, ie with the most recent job first and working backwards.

2. The from-to dates are given in years only and are placed in the right-hand margin.

3. As previously mentioned, Henry worked for a while in a stationer's. He was 26 when he completed his BTEC Diploma, as can be inferred from his personal information. But he does not mention either fact. Why? It is simply not relevant. In any case it is too long ago. Any job that was undertaken more than eight years ago should be looked at carefully. If it is unconnected with the current application, jettison it. And even for more recent jobs, if they are not relevant, axe them. If the work experience section has conspicuous gaps, you can head it 'Selected achievements' or 'Employment highlights'. The function of the

Henry Norton
23 Chingford Lane,
Walthamstow E17 4AM
(0208) 123 4567
henry.norton@anyserver.com

PROFILE
Highly professional travel consultant with 7 years' experience and excellent knowledge of booking package holidays to long-haul and short-haul destinations. Smart appearance and excellent interpersonal/communication skills in one-to-one, telephone or e-mail contact.

AREAS OF EXPERTISE INCLUDE:
- Assessment of client needs
- Customer service/satisfaction
- Excellent knowledge of geography, airport operations, travel-related health issues, passports, visas and other documentation
- Skilled at CRS
- Above-average account retention
- Excellent PC skills
- Able to work to achieve targets and incentives in a fast-paced environment
- Trilingual, English/French/Spanish

PROFESSIONAL EXPERIENCE

Sunquest Travel, Luton   2001–present
Travel consultant
Achievements:
- Selected as one of 25 travel agents company-wide to attend training course in travel marketing
- Rapidly acquired knowledge of CRS system to book personal and business travel
- Advised customers on travel products and services, particularly 4 and 5 star holidays to discerning and knowledgeable clients travelling to European and worldwide destinations
- Achieved high success rate at year-on-year booking
- Worked as part of a team recognized as 'Business Travel Management Company 2005' at that year's Business Travel World Awards for the eighth time in ten years
- Provided first-class customer service from inquiry to sale closure and follow-up
- Regularly attended training sessions and conferences

Greenhouse Travel, Humberton   1998–2001
Travel consultant
Achievements:
- Quickly mastered dealing with tour operators via viewdata
- Worked difficult itineraries
- Worked in both leisure and corporate travel
- Met company targets in 90% of cases and exceeded them in 70%
- Trained in money transfer

EDUCATION
BTEC National Diploma in Travel and Tourism, 1998

PERSONAL
D.o.b. 27.3.72
Married, no children

REFERENCES
Available on request

CV is not to detail your life history, it is to get you an interview. Henry's stint at the stationer's, and his part-time jobs working in factories before that, will not help him.

4. It mentions the word 'achievements' prominently in the 'Professional experience' section. The reason is this: things actually done and achieved are extremely powerful. They are by far the most important focus of interest for an employer, ranking above when something happened or who it was done for.

5. Henry has taken his experience at work and extracted from it not just his responsibilities, but those areas where he took his responsibilities – which anyone has purely by the fact of being employed – and turned them into successes.

6. Henry's most recent job is given the most attention in terms of length. This makes sense as the recruiter is going to want to talk to him about what he has shown he can do yesterday rather than what he was capable of five years ago. It also suggests that Henry's career is gathering pace.

Education

Where should you stick your education? That's not a rude question. Should it be proudly at the top of the CV or among the optional candidates at the end? It all depends on who you are and what job you are trying to get. If you have just left school, college or university, your educational experience is going to loom large. Your potential employer may be keen to hire recent graduates and will wish to see exactly what your educational attainments are. This means you can give plenty of detail of curricula, theses and grades. However, if you have been in the world of work for 20 years, your education is of little interest to an employer and should go in skeletal form near the bottom of the CV. What you have achieved since leaving full-time education is obviously more indicative of your value.

Another thing to bear in mind is that higher qualifications imply lower ones. If you have only got GCSEs, fine. If, however, you have a university degree, it is superfluous to mention your GCSEs, or even your A levels, unless they are spectacularly good. A recruiter will simply assume they were taken at the usual time and is unlikely to be interested in how many there were and what grades they were. The same applies to a Masters degree or a PhD. The higher qualification makes mention of any lower ones redundant.

Where it is felt necessary to mention more in the way of academic attainment, for example as a recent graduate or as someone with professional qualifications or other post-graduate training, the section should be organized in reverse chronological order, like your work experience section.

Although what you include should be truthful and accurate, omission is not a crime. If, for example, you did a degree course but got a very low mark, you do not need to mention the mark. If you attended a university but had to leave half-way through, the university can still appear on your CV, as long as you have got a good explanation if the incident comes up at interview. And perhaps most importantly for older employees, it is not necessary to give the dates of your qualifications; they only go to emphasize your age. You will not be taken away and charged with CV violation if your education section reads simply:

> Education
>
> BA (Hons) Modern English Studies, University of Stirling, First Class, winner of the Dean Jones Prize

This is a real example from the CV of a 52-year-old woman, and looks perfectly acceptable without dates.

Education extras

The education section may include other information that could be relevant. In applying for work in the academic or scientific fields, for example, it may list scholarships and awards that will boost your attractiveness to the employer. Professional qualifications can also be listed in the education section. Affiliations to professional bodies or guilds can be put here, as can various certificates of training or mention of attendance at special courses and seminars.

Finally, the education section can be the place to mention the all-important computer skills that continue to dominate working life. Different jobs and professions will require you to have an understanding of different software packages, and if you are conversant with these it is as well to mention you know they exist, or have been trained to use them. If you are applying for a job more closely related to IT, your technical proficiencies should have a section of their own (entitled 'computer efficiency' or 'computer skills' or 'technical expertise') much higher up in the priority list.

In some otherwise excellent CVs the sense of anticlimax given by the interests section can be truly paralyzing. Here are some things you simply should never list in your interests section:

- reading
- cooking
- television
- family
- children

These 'interests' are not at all interesting. They are the default activities of most human beings and are on a par with sleeping. If, however, these are all you can come up with then at least try to vary it a little, for example:

- reading about new developments in science and technology
- southern Malaysian cookery
- camping at weekends with family and children

As far as television is concerned, remind yourself of the words of Noel Coward: 'Television is not for watching, it is for being on.'

Sports can be a valuable addition to your interests section. Remember that the function of everything on the CV is to get you an interview, or the job. The interests section is no different. Listing sports can indicate, subliminally, qualities you might be able to demonstrate as an employee, specifically:

- Team sports (football, netball, etc): good interpersonal skills, ability to delegate/lead.

INTERESTS

- Individual competitive sports (cycling, climbing, etc): determination, aggression, self-motivation.
- Cerebral sports (chess, bridge, etc): intelligence, curiosity, analytical skills.

Other achievements worth including are anything where you have won the endorsement of your peers by being appointed or elected to a position, such as becoming president of a club. These are valuable because, unlike most of what will appear on your CV, they contain a suggestion of the objective opinion of others. This can speak volumes.

A final category of things worth mentioning includes awards or distinctions. If you play the tuba badly and have not picked it up for ten years, do not mention it. If you have just passed your Grade 8 with distinction, do mention it. Also mention languages spoken, giving the level of attainment, where possible with a recent examination mark.

And be prepared to elaborate on what you have included. If you claim to be able to speak Hungarian fluently but in reality it is more than a little rusty, you do not want to find yourself fretting a few minutes before the interview that there will be a member on the panel from Budapest.

References

Most CV experts now advise you not to give the names and contact details of referees on the CV itself. This is good advice. There are three main reasons for not giving them:

- Employers won't check them before the interview because it is too much paperwork. References are usually only taken up after a candidate has been selected.
- References are in any case of little value because anyone the candidate has nominated is bound to put in a favourable report. So, again, they are not going to be taken up at the pre-interview stage.
- Employers assume that references are there if they need them. They do not need to be taking up valuable space on your CV.

By putting 'references available on request' you are going as far as any employer wants at the CV stage.

Endorsements

Endorsements, however, can be effective in the CV itself. In the example on page 33, the CV includes actual quotations from people in support of the application. Consider for a moment the psychology of this. Here we have what purports to be objective third-party opinion singing the praises of the candidate. It feels very impressive. The recruiter now has a choice. On the one hand they can accept this is legal, decent, honest and truthful, which means a very favourable result for the candidate. On the other hand they can request the contact details of the maths teacher or shop manager who has made the statement, and investigate. The percentage which goes for option B is always going to be a tiny minority and, assuming the quotes are real, the applicant has no cause to worry. Endorsements placed in this way can therefore be extremely effective.

One point to note, however: if you do include reference contacts or endorsements, tell the referees or endorsers about it, so they are not perplexed and/or annoyed by receiving a letter or, worse, a phone call from someone they do not know. Contact them and apprise them of what direction your career is taking, the sort of work you are looking for, and what any potential employer is going to be looking for from you. This sort of advance warning is worthwhile.

Presentation

Finally, a note on presentation. When printing out your CV, use A4 white paper of the best quality available (though not so heavy it feels like a certificate of merit). If sending it through the post, use a matching envelope – a C4 envelope is best, since this will avoid having to fold your CV. Make sure you use a good printer. Poor quality print is not only hard to read and looks sloppy, but it is hard for machines to scan. Do not present it on coloured paper, and do not use any fancy graphics. Do not use very large or very small type or unusual fonts.

Finally, do not send a photograph unless they specifically ask for one. You may be beautiful, but that it is unlikely to make a difference.

CV databases

CVs gather dust as efficiently as any other household item. Once you have written your CV you have to get recruiters to read it. One of the commonest ways to do this nowadays is to post it online. That way you do not go to the employers: they come to you.

There are two main ways to do this:

- Go to an employer's website and post it there.
- Use an online CV bank that exists for this purpose, where employers can come looking for you.

The first method will often be used in connection with specific vacancies at particular companies. To search the current vacancies you just go to the company careers page, find vacancies that you are qualified for, and add your CV to the pool.

The second method is more scattershot. The problem is finding the right site. Many books on CVs will give you 'some useful addresses' at this point, but any book more than two years old that includes web addresses and uses the word 'useful' will be running foul of the Trades Descriptions Act: most of them will have ceased to exist, be changed out of all recognition or will be supplanted by newer, better ones that you should really be looking at instead.

The way to find the right CV bank today, when you are reading this book, is to use a search engine. Type in a phrase such as "post your CV" or "job bank" (using double quotes) and you will then get a range of sites offering you this service. (Tip: limit your search to websites from the country you are living in, unless you are looking for jobs abroad.) The most useful are meta-sites: sites that offer lists of sites ordered by specialism, such as agriculture or teaching. If you want to go straight to these niche sites, then try typing in "post your CV" followed by your job title (eg "post your CV" teaching.)

An alternative method is to use a directory such as Yahoo or Lycos. Internet directories are just like paper directories: they show you where to find services, goods, love, entertainment and so on. You may find, however, that using a directory will only lead you by a slightly more circuitous route to the same place you would have arrived at by just typing in "post your CV".

Uploading

Once you are at the right site, you will be invited to upload the CV you have already created. In the friendlier sites this will be in the form of a Word document, so you can do it in a couple of mouse-clicks. Other sites have forms to fill in, rather jauntily called wizards. This can take up to half an hour to do, which may be off-putting. (Tip: if you are able to cut and paste from a CV stored on your hard drive it will speed things up.) The result is that your CV is shoehorned into the format the site wants, which is fine, since by coming to such a site employers do not expect egregious displays of individuality. Unfortunately all your formatting and font choices will disappear.

When posting your CV you should bear in mind that it will need renewing regularly. In some databases it is possible to search by the newest postings, which will mean that if your CV hasn't been renewed recently it will come down in the searchlist.

It is also possible to have more than one CV in a database, with the wording changed slightly, to increase your chances of success. More than about five CVs makes you a 'CV spammer' though, so do not do that – it is not nice.

Web CVs

Another alternative is to publish your CV online as a web page. This is not as difficult as you might think. You can use the web-publishing software that comes free with your operating system, or something flashier like Macromedia Dreamweaver. You do not need to pay for a domain name or hosting either, if you do not want to. Simply use the free web space given to you by your server (all servers provide free web space, and the best ones provide it free of advertisements). Instead of sending your CV as an attachment you then direct the employer to a personal web page, which means they do not have to risk downloading a virus by opening an attachment. You simply say something in your covering e-mail such as 'You can see my CV by following this link.'

Confidentiality, spam and spiders

What about confidentiality? Your contact details are there for all to see, aren't they? Not necessarily. Some CV banks will give you the option of withholding contact details, which are then only given out to employers on request. This protects you from programs called 'spiders' which crawl across the internet looking for e-mail addresses to add to spamming lists. Some CV banks will even stop employers from seeing your details until you personally give the go-ahead.

The best approach, if you are worried, is to read the site's privacy policy, which should be given as a link at the bottom of the page. If you do not like what you read (or there isn't a policy there), move on.

If you are particularly frightened of spam, though, the best thing to do is to protect yourself against it by other means – setting up your e-mail program to block unwanted senders, having more than one e-mail address (one of which acts as a foil to attract junk), and choosing a good server. If you have got a server that takes spam seriously and filters it out intelligently by noting the traffic bulk mailers generate, it is worth its weight in e-gold.

CV DATABASES

It might be as well to reflect, though, that many of us give out personal information on the internet all the time by shopping, downloading programs or filling in online forms. Even in the snail-world that we inhabit in the meantime, our names, addresses and phone numbers are available for all to see in a free document called The Phone Book.

E-mailing CVs

If you have your CV in electronic form, stored as a document on your computer (which you should have in the modern job market) then one thing you are going to want to do is e-mail it to employers. In an increasing number of job adverts now you will see a request to e-mail CVs as part of an application.

If you are applying for an advertised position, take a lead from the employer. If they ask you to send your CV as an attachment, do so. A Word attachment is fine. To be extra safe you could send the CV as a plain-text attachment without formatting, since the CV may be scanned electronically and plain text will eliminate any potential problems at their end. You can do this by creating it in ordinary word-processing software and then saving it with a file name ending '.txt' (use the drop-down menu in Word, for example, that says 'Save as type'). Alternatively you can use a program such as Notepad that only generates plain text.

If the employer says simply 'Send your CV', you have three options. You can either attach your CV, send it in the body of the e-mail, or do both. The best bet is to do both. The reason is that many employers do not like opening attachments, even if they are requesting CVs. If they have just had a big virus scare they may only look at candidates who have sent their CVs in the body of the e-mail.

Doing both also allows you to send the CV in two different formats: a formatted one for the body of the e-mail and a plain-text one for the attachment. The plain-text version will be useful to put straight into a database. Make it clear in your covering e-mail what you have done and in which format each has been sent.

And here we come to a crucial point: if you e-mail your CV, employers will usually store it in an electronic database, not print it out and keep it in a filing cabinet. This gives them space for an extra rubber plant. It also gives them the capability of searching the database by keyword to look for the best person for a job. The fact is, your CV may never be read by a human. It may be read by a robot.

Keywords

Keyword searching has been standard in the USA for some time. Now it is being used increasingly in large companies in the UK. What happens is that the computer looks for particular words that indicate a suitable applicant. These will whittle down a pile of 1000 CVs into a pile of 50, which can then be read by a human.

The upshot is that it is wise to sprinkle your CV liberally with the right keywords. These are usually nouns and noun-phrases. For a secretary, the keywords would be:

> *word processing, shorthand, organizational skills, office management, spreadsheets, planning, co-ordination*

For a computer programmer they would be:

> *mainframe, PC, Mac, Unix, Networks, Windows, SQL, NT, TCP/IP, server, diagnostics, project management*

Some books suggest you collect all your keywords together and put them in a box at the end of your CV, but this is not really necessary as long as these key job-related nouns appear somewhere in your CV.

Scannability

In order to be able to search CVs, employers will in some cases try to convert your paper CV, if you have sent them one, into an e-CV.

They do this by scanning it into a computer using a technology called Optical Character Recognition, which recognizes the individual letters (and some formatting such as paragraph marks) and converts them into a plain-text file. You need to make this as easy for the machine as possible, so some good tips are:

- Put your name at the top on a separate line. Do not call your CV 'CV' or anything at all. Lead with your name.
- Do not use serif fonts. Use plain fonts such as Arial or Verdana.
- Put phone numbers on their own line.
- Leave a space between sections.
- Avoid formatting such as graphics, tables, italics, shading or borders. Bullet points are OK.
- Do not fold the paper. Send it in a large envelope (the crease confuses the scanner).

One final point on electronic CVs – the title of the document on your computer is likely to be something like 'CV.doc'. That's fine, though it could be a little more informative for your potential employer: JamesGoldburnCV.doc is better. What you should guard against is anything you have named the CV that you wouldn't want an employer to see: 'OldCV.doc', for instance.

Part Two

Application Forms

Application forms: the basics

It is nice to start off on a positive. So, let's just say that, whatever else they may be, application forms are a great leveller. Everyone has to fill in the same boxes.

Some more good news: whether you take the lead after that is largely up to you. Of course, one candidate may have more experience to draw on, but another may be more skilled at drawing on the little experience they have. Some have excellent qualifications but make elementary mistakes and lower their chances of success. It is often the way you do it that counts.

The more adaptable you are, the better your chances of success. Forms can vary from a single sheet to something the size of a small book. They can be designed to be completed online or filled in at home by hand and posted. They can be intended to accompany a CV or stand alone instead of one. Each form must be looked at carefully to see what sort of information it is trying to elicit.

That last point should be stressed, even though it may seem obvious. You might be surprised at how many people put the same information on each form, rushing through them as if they will not be read with any great attention. The assumption seems to be that the application form is the poor cousin of the CV, and that there is no reason to be diligent or professional. But the need to sell yourself is just as great. You may be among dozens or even hundreds of candidates applying for the same post. Any competitive edge you can exploit will be the difference between success and failure.

Employers, when looking at completed forms in which everyone has essentially the same starting point and the same chances, will be doing three things:

- looking for conspicuous faults, failings or absences
- ticking off requirements
- noting outstanding strengths

The first activity involves looking for reasons to disqualify candidates by looking for messiness, poor layout, hastiness, poor spelling, poor grammar, incomprehensibility, and omissions. The circular file may well beckon for anyone guilty of these elementary mistakes.

The second activity involves finding out whether the candidate fulfils the job and/or person specification of the original advertisement. In most cases, in a competitive job market, all the essential requirements and most of the 'preferable' requirements should be met. If some of the bases are uncovered, it could be (and often is) goodbye.

That leaves a much smaller pile. Now it is time to compare the strong candidates. Who can offer the most to the company? Those bringing added value by demonstrating skills or achievements in a persuasive manner will be allowed residence in the smallest pile of all – the interview short list.

Messiness

You should present your form in the same way as you would present yourself at interview: tidy and smartly dressed. The human resources manager is not eccentric or unconventional. He or she is conservative, cautious, humourless and allergic to risk. A scrawl – even if writing skills are not part of the job specification – will send your application to the reject pile. If it is at all difficult to read, it won't get read. Crossings-out, correction fluid and pieces of paper pasted into the form are likewise to be avoided. They indicate one or more of the following:

- This applicant doesn't know their own mind.
- This applicant is not skilled in careful planning and preparation.
- This applicant is scruffy in person.
- This applicant has low standards and doesn't see anything wrong with them.

Writing and typing

One way to avoid an appearance of messiness, if your handwriting is not everything it could be, is to write (by hand) in capital letters. Although experts contend that lower-case writing is easier to read (since the letter shapes protrude above and below the middle line and are thus easier to distinguish from one another), capital letters are neater (a non-expert's term). Most people writing in lower case slip naturally into cursive. Indeed, if they do not, the result will look very stilted, which is not always easy for others to decipher. Your non-cursive capital lettering will probably have better definition and therefore better readability than your lower-case writing.

Completing by hand can give you an advantage, if you do it well. Good, neat, accurate handwriting is desirable for many jobs. An alternative though is to type your answers. In the first part of the form, where you give personal, educational and work experience details, this should be avoided. It is extremely difficult to type into the boxes on an application, especially using a computer. Somehow, when it prints out, the writing never fits convincingly into the boxes and the result looks careless. Completing the first part by hand is perfectly acceptable.

The second, more challenging part of the form, where you have to give your reasons for applying for the post or make a 'covering statement' of some kind, may be typed, even if the first part has been completed by hand. It is common for forms to ask candidates to attach an additional sheet at this point, so you can simply write on the form 'see attached sheet' and attach your covering statement, immaculately typed, to the form. If you do attach a sheet, make sure you title it appropriately and put your name and contact details at the bottom of each additional sheet.

Alternatively, with a little care in spacing (practise printing on some rough paper beforehand) you can print onto the form where it gives you space – typically a large area, often a whole page. This is a difficult manoeuvre but it looks good.

Online forms

We are all increasingly familiar with the online form, for shopping, downloading software and so on. It is another common way of applying for jobs, though such forms will typically be used only by larger companies who can afford the comparatively sophisticated web design that makes them possible. They will usually follow the format of conventional paper forms, with fields in which to type your answers for personal details, work experience, covering statement and so on. As with any other online form, you can usually navigate through the form from field to field by using the 'Tab' key.

In recognition of the fact that application forms will often not be completed at a single sitting, some online forms offer you the chance to save your form in an uncompleted state in the employer's own database; only when you have finished and are satisfied with it are you invited to press a button that notifies the employer that the completed form is ready to read. You may even receive reminders by e-mail that an uncompleted form is still waiting, lonely and unfilled, for your final touches.

Pdfs

Pdf stands for portable document format. If you haven't encountered pdfs in your job-seeking career so far, it is highly likely you will soon.

Pdfs were developed (by the software company Adobe) to reproduce, on a computer screen, the exact appearance and dimensions of any paper document. The idea is that you can view and print out the document, and it will look the same as it would do if you'd been handed a copy. It is like being faxed, although no-one has to do the sending.

Pdf application forms go one step further. They allow users to fill in the form on screen, and, once happy with the result, print it out, or even send it to an employer as an e-mail attachment.

As you can probably see, this is a big advantage. You can make as many attempts as you want and keep going back to make improvements. You do not even need a stamp.

It is a big advantage to the employer too, which is why they are so popular. It is relatively simple to make a pdf out of an already-existing paper form, whereas it is more difficult and expensive to create a true online form with all the functionality (automatic data entry, re-submission protocols, etc) that users have come to expect.

If the recruiter has specified that it is possible to apply online via a pdf, go to the appropriate web page and click on the link for the application form. This will open the pdf. You'll see a little hand appear where the mouse pointer usually is. If you click the mouse and hold it down, this hand turns into a little fist. By moving the mouse up or down you can scroll up and down in the document, or in some cases side-to-side.

When you get to a field where you are allowed to add text, the little hand will change to a symbol that looks like an elongated capital 'I'. You can then fill in all your details.

A word of warning: it is not always possible to save pdfs on your computer. Some programs, especially the free ones, won't let you. You may come across a message like this:

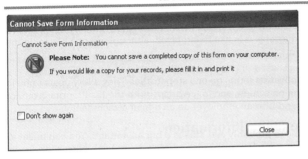

This means that you can't save the information, and if you exit the form and go back later, it will be lost. If you want to take a long time over the application, it is probably best to print it out and fill it out by hand, or fill it out and print it one page at a time.

In the best-case scenario, however, you may see a message like this:

This means that your computer can save the information you have completed. Just click 'Save as' and save to your hard drive or a floppy. When you re-open the pdf, make sure you select 'Open with Adobe Reader' (or any other reader you are using), otherwise the result will look like gibberish.

If the pdf has saved and opened correctly, that means you can send it to the employer as an e-mail attachment. Just click on the e-mail button on the top toolbar.

To view and print pdfs you need a couple of basic things:

- A reader – most commonly Adobe Acrobat, software that enables you to view pdfs, which you can download free of charge.
- A printer.
- In some cases, 'extracting' software that will let you download compressed files and expand them after download. WinZip is a type of extracting program and you can download a trial program free of charge from the WinZip website.

Not enough information

The boxes on most forms are the size they are for a reason: the employer expects you to be able to fill the given space with information. The larger the box, the more skills and achievements expected. If you feel that you are right for the job but you can't find enough to say to fill up the space on a particular question, it is usually a question of re-examining your skills and achievements to find something. You may be neglecting to mention voluntary work, for instance (see page 88) or 'transferable skills' from other jobs (see page 80).

If you are given the opportunity to continue on a separate sheet of paper, typically in a 'covering statement', do so. Employers who offer this provision are doing so out of a genuine desire to find the right candidate. For you, this is an opportunity to shine, and should never be passed over. The difference between two first-rate applications may be very slight, and the one who has written at greater length, as long as that greater length contains valuable additional information, will win the day.

Too much information

On the other hand, a common fault is to squeeze in too much information, especially in the early part of the form. An employer doesn't necessarily want to know about every exam you have ever taken (see page 41). Similarly, not every job you have ever done is likely to be relevant (see page 38). If in doubt, use the following general rules. Write as much as you can that will:

- not overflow the space provided unless an additional sheet is suggested
- bring to bear all your relevant skills in a concise, concrete manner without being too wordy or elaborate
- avoid repetition

That way you are unlikely to go wrong.

Orthographically and syntactically challenged

Poor spelling and grammar are obviously not the worst crimes in the world, and in jobs that involve little if any paperwork, the capacity for perfection in this area is completely irrelevant. Even so, employers will still mark you down for any slip they notice. Why? Simply because, in the absence of anything else to go on, poor spelling and grammar indicate someone who may be careless, inattentive to detail or poorly educated.

Good spelling and grammar are therefore absolutely vital in every part of your job application, from the CV to the application form to the covering letter. If you are writing part of it by hand and you know your spelling or grammar could be improved, give it to someone who prides themselves on their spelling abilities and get them to check it. If you are typing part of it, use a spellcheck and grammar check as a first defence. Again, if you are concerned that your spelling or grammar is weak, you will probably need additional measures, as such mechanical checks are not foolproof. For example, a machine will not pick up what it sees as 'alternative' correct words which are in reality wrong, as in the sentence 'I sore a nod thing.' It is a good idea to have a dictionary at hand. Poor spacing, capitalization and punctuation will also often slip through. So read it through carefully and get someone else to check it if you are still not sure.

Repetition

Do not duplicate information. The form is trying to draw out different aspects of your career and personal qualities. Even if the form seems to be inviting you to say the same thing twice, resist the temptation. Take, for instance, the following two questions, appearing on the same form:

- What skills do you have that make you suitable for this post?
- Give an example where you demonstrated good interpersonal skills.

You may find that you have answered the first without leaving yourself anything to answer the second with. Read the form carefully and note where there might be problem areas, as in the case above. Then formulate your answers so you are giving completely new replies or examples in each field. For the first question above, for instance, you would probably list good interpersonal skills as one of your basic skills, accompanying this with an example such as 'encouraged and motivated community project volunteers'. For the second question you will give a new example of the same skill, probably in more detail.

Disregarding instructions

This is another basic fault. If the form says jump, then jump. Do not leave any blanks, fail to give examples where requested, miss any aspect of the job description or person specification (see page 66), leave boxes unticked, or fail to sign or date it at the bottom. These sins will count heavily against you. If any area of the form is simply not relevant (eg 'Tel. mobile' if you do not have a mobile phone), put 'N/A'.

Another common mistake concerns the attachment or non-attachment of CVs. If it says on the form 'Do not attach your CV', then do not. That is a serious personnel-irritant and may cost you the job.

AGGRESSIVE TOY MARKETER WANTED

Do they want aggressive people or people who market aggressive toys? Probably best to read the rest of the advertisement.

The job specification is your initial source of information about what the company wants. Later, you can supplement it with other information: research into the company's history, its promotional materials or its website, and, of course, the application form itself. But the original advertisement should always be kept in mind as a primary source of information when applying for the job.

Let's look at a typical advertisement:

Position:
Logistics manager in charge of delivering telecommunication services to an expanding international client base

Job description:
- Linking the supply chain with nominated internal customers
- Ensuring excellent levels of communication
- Seeking to improve service and performance
- Project direction that drives continuous improvement in service coupled with cost reduction

Personal Qualifications:
Essential
- A sound knowledge of the telecommunication market
- Account management experience
- Excellent numeracy and IT skills

Preferred
- At least 10 years within the logistic and distributions fields
- A bachelor's degree or higher

THE SPECIFICATION

You will notice that this has two main parts, the job specification and the person specification. Within the second category are two more divisions: what is essential and what is preferred.

Job specification

In the preceding example there are four main responsibilities, describing the life and times of a logistics manager. As previously mentioned, one of the main activities of the human resources manager who is looking at your form will be ticking off requirements. Unless you address all of them in your application, the likelihood is that you will fail.

Whereabouts in the form you address these requirements depends very much on the form itself. If there is a lot of space for your work experience, address them there, giving concrete examples of how you have 'improved service and performance' or 'ensured excellent levels of communication' (see page 35 for more details). If there is not enough room in the work experience section, which may seem designed only for basic details such as dates and addresses, give the information they require in the 'covering statement' section (see page 79). Wherever you put it, make sure it goes in. If you get the opportunity, give it in more than one section, as long as the examples you are providing are new, additional examples.

Many forms now are organized so as to make this process easier. Instead of leaving you to work out for yourself from the job advertisement what they are looking for, the form will have different sections for you to demonstrate each skill or achievement. So in the example above there might be discrete parts of the form in which you are asked to demonstrate 'project direction skills' and so on.

Person specification

The person specification is a guide to the qualities needed to take on the role in the job description. You need to show those skills and attributes in the most attractive manner possible. Again, the section available to you to demonstrate those qualities can vary. It could be the 'covering statement' or another section with a question such as: 'What are your best qualities?' 'What skills and experience do you have that make you suitable for this job?' or 'Please give examples of your problem-solving activities in the logistic and distribution fields.'

The person specification will often have two parts: essential and preferred. If possible, try to demonstrate both essential and preferred skills. If not possible, still address them, but give an alternative or 'transferable' skill. For example, the person specification above says that a degree is preferred. Someone who did not have one could stress the fact that, although they do not have a degree, they do have a relevant professional qualification or a proven track record. If you can demonstrate that you have saved money, increased profitability or cut the time taken to do something, this will often be favoured over academic achievement. Put yourself in the shoes of a personnel manager. Which would you prefer – a new graduate with some big ideas, or someone who has just saved his or her previous employer a large sum of money?

Take your time

Once you have got the advertisement and the form, take your time. You are taking an important step in your working life, so think of the time you'll spend on the form as an investment. A day or two spent over it is not disproportionate given that you are seeking employment that may last for years.

What you are going to do is similar to what you did when creating your CV: to examine your skills and achievements and present them in such a way to make the employer want to find out more at an interview. Remember that a full and detailed examination of your skills is a valuable exercise, even if, on any one occasion, you do not get the job. It will:

- help you with the next application

- be invaluable at interview, if you get one
- give you confidence in your abilities

The effort is unlikely to be wasted.

Copies

Bear in mind the words of Ernest Hemingway: 'The only writers are re-writers.' After you have completed the form it is highly likely that you'll go back to it and notice something that could be done better. If you have written straight onto it in the full flush of composition, you won't be able to change it without crossings-out or correction fluid, which look ugly.

The best solution therefore is to make a copy of the form and practise on it. Photocopying it is the easiest, but you can also make a handwritten mock-up of it if you are careful to leave the right spaces to tailor your answers to. An even better solution is to scan it in and print it out, and then you can have unlimited copies.

You need to take time to think, to edit, to polish.

Personal details

Name, rank and serial number

This half of the form is the standard information that everyone has to give. You can breeze through most of it, cutting and pasting from a document on your hard drive (if completing it on a computer). It will include name, address, telephone number, e-mail address, date of birth, and possibly other details such as National Insurance number or job reference number.

One warning: be careful with your phone and e-mail contact information. It is quite likely that you will be asked to supply a work phone number (or daytime phone number). If you have to answer calls from a recruiter and your boss is listening (or worse, if they pick up the phone), it could be awkward if they do not know about it (or even if they do). The solution that some adopt is to give a mobile phone number that can be easily monitored, so that they can choose whether or not to accept the call; you can have an answerphone message on it promising to 'ring straight back' so the recruiter will not feel you are making their job difficult.

E-mail is another tricky area: some employers are able to monitor staff e-mails. The best solution is to give your home e-mail address rather than your work one, if possible. Do not then ruin it by checking your home address at work using webmail: webmail uses internet web pages like any other website and can be monitored by your boss. You may then have some explaining to do.

Sex, disability and ethnic origin

Employers may state somewhere on the form that they are opposed to discrimination on the grounds of age, culture, disability, race, sex, HIV status, marital status, nationality, religion or sexual orientation. They are, however, not legally prohibited from discrimination in all of these areas: discrimination on the grounds of age, HIV status or the fact that you are pregnant is, at the time of writing, legal (you cannot be sacked from your job because you are pregnant but as the law stands you have no legal redress if you believe you were not recruited because you were pregnant).

In Britain, however, there are Acts of Parliament that protect candidates from discrimination on grounds of race, sex, sexuality or disability; they are the Race Relations Act, The Sex Discrimination Act, the Employment Equality (Sexual Orientation) Act, the Equal Pay Act and the Disability Discrimination Act. Employers who discriminate against candidates at interview for any of these reasons can theoretically be taken to a tribunal, but few successful cases are ever brought, since employers can quite easily claim that there were other defects in the application that barred the candidate.

The Department of Trade and Industry has recently published a draft bill to outlaw age-based discrimination, which may well make it illegal at some point in the near future to discriminate against someone on the grounds of age, whether in recruitment or as a member of staff.

Accompanying your application form is likely to be a document in which you are invited to state your ethnic origin and/or any disabilities. This is theoretically unrelated to the application per se, being a method employers use to monitor whether their equal opportunities policies are being carried out. You may also be asked to state whether you carry out a caring role for children or relatives.

A note on disability: some forms will ask you to say whether you have a disability (as defined under the Disability Discrimination Act); others will say that disability need only be declared if you are short-listed for interview. It varies. In neither case should it affect your application, as such a thing would be illegal.

A note on ethnicity: it is not essential to be absolutely accurate. The form will sometimes advise you to tick the box which you consider most closely approximates to a description of your ethnic origin. If you wish to give further information there will often be a space provided to state your ethnic group. In any case, your compliance is not a legal requirement, though absent or misleading information will not improve your chances of success.

Education and training

Again, study details can be pasted in. Forms differ widely in the level of detail required. Some will give separate boxes for everything from secondary school upwards, requiring names and addresses, exams, marks and dates. Others will give one box marked 'Education'. In the latter case it is fair to assume that less information is required, and it is a good rule to put in what will comfortably fit in the box. If it is about an inch deep, put your highest and most recent qualification first, with name of institution, brief details of exam passed (eg six GSCEs) and dates, followed by the next highest if applicable – and that will suffice. Two inches deep, think about giving a third where applicable or expanding on the qualifications (that doesn't mean making up extra ones). There will often be a section for 'Other training'; again, fill in as much detail as there is room for.

Close to the education section there is sometimes a separate question about proficiency in languages. If this is the case it is a safe bet that the employer regards this as important, a benchmark of your intellectual abilities and general employability. You should treat it seriously, therefore, and make a distinction in your replies between basic, working and fluent, giving details of any examinations taken. Do not lie! Being caught out in this area could prove embarrassing at an interview. Another distinction you can make is that between spoken and written proficiency, which might well be sharply different.

It is at this point that forms start getting tricky. Understandably so, since this is the area employers are most keen to examine.

A typical form will give sections for dates, employer details (name alone is sometimes sufficient but usually name and address are required), position, responsibilities and achievements, reason for leaving and final salary. If there is simply a space for 'work experience' with no guidelines as to what to put in it, restrict yourself to employer name, dates (in years), position and achievements. Leave out the reason for leaving and final salary.

A note on your 'position': you may have held more than one position at any one company, so give the most senior first, also listing, in reverse chronological order, any former positions (if there is enough room). If you were a junior member of staff, try not to put 'junior' in front of the position; also avoid using the word 'assistant'. Both terms subtly downplay your role. For a shop assistant, for example, try putting 'retail worker'.

There is no need to give every job you have ever held; as with your CV, you should think hard about including anything more than eight years ago. Even for more recent employment, do not include it if it is completely irrelevant (except if it is your current or last job). Employers want to read about what is pertinent to them, and what will make you a valuable employee.

Now is the time to attend to the basic details of your career. There is a balance to be struck here; this is not necessarily the place to start giving the hard sell in terms of statistics, achievements or value. Do not forget that most applications contain a very nasty sting in the tail (from the point of view of the applicant): the 'covering statement' (see page 79). That is the place for the personal pitch; the work experience section is where you put, in the most positive way possible, your duties, responsibilities, commitments, supervisory experience, and so on. Of course, if there is no 'covering statement' section in the form, that changes things. It is then the work experience section that should contain elements of the hard sell.

The work experience section need not be purely factual, however. There are subtler ways of selling yourself. Consider the following two descriptions:

> *Bridgestone Inc, 1997–98*
>
> *Account Manager*
>
> *Experience included developing consumer packaging, working on brand awareness, introducing new production methods, installing computer systems, sales, displays and publicity.*

> *Bridgestone Inc, 1997–98*
>
> *Senior Account Manager*
>
> *Developed cutting-edge consumer packaging. Achieved consistently high targets for brand awareness. Successfully introduced DTP and database management at all levels. Worked with leading advertising agencies to create high-impact campaigns.*

There are only 9 more words in the second one but the differences are noticeable:

- The job title sounds more impressive. If it is a senior position, say so.
- The description uses active verbs in the past, rather than the present continuous. This gives the subconscious impression that the things mentioned are done, finished, achieved.

- 'Working on brand awareness' – which gives the impression of struggling to do something difficult – is changed to 'Achieved consistently high targets for brand awareness', which is more powerful.

- Instead of one long sentence which rather tails off, it is made up of short, punchy sentences.

- 'Installing computer systems' is changed to give both a higher level of detail and a value-judgement – 'successfully introduced'. It sounds more attractive and, if necessary, the candidate will be able to back it up with more detail at interview.

In summary: be dynamic, enthusiastic and bold. Your form has to begin to get into gear at this point. It has to say strongly 'I am the best candidate.'

Dates

Employers are heartless creatures. They want to find your weaknesses and reject you. One of the weaknesses they are especially averse to is unemployment. If they find you have been unemployed for too long they will mark you down (and possibly out). If this sounds overly harsh, consider the following question, found on many forms in the work experience section:

> 'Please give details of any breaks in employment.'

This is extremely devious. What it really means is 'Please say when, and for how long, and why, you were unemployed, and you better have a pretty good excuse.' It aims to circumvent your trick of making your employment dates look as good as possible by only giving year dates. But do not let it worry you. The interpretation of the word 'break' is still in your hands. There is normally a break of some kind between jobs. A month is not uncommon, so you do not need to declare that as a break. Four months may mean you have had a period of enforced unemployment, and the decision is thus in your hands whether to draw it to their attention or not.

EMPLOYMENT HISTORY

As a rule of thumb, anything up to four months need not be declared. Anything over four may be declared, but it is not absolutely necessary. It is a risk you take, gambling on whether they will find out from a previous employer that a break has occurred.

One point to make here is that unemployment can be explained in a number of ways if you choose to declare it. It may even count in your favour. You can give details of voluntary work you have undertaken during the period of the break. You can give reasons such as having taken time out for pregnancy/childcare. You can give details of foreign travel or service overseas. All of these give you the opportunity to show the acquisition of valuable new skills, exciting personal development or real achievement. Just because you were unemployed it doesn't necessarily mean you spent all the time watching TV.

The employer's next question is another trap for the unwary:

> 'What are/were the reasons for leaving or wishing to leave your current/last employment?'

As pointed out in the CV section of this book, most reasons for leaving a job tend to reflect badly on your loyalties to or relationship with previous employers. If you are forced to declare one, though, it must be done – and it must be truthful. This doesn't mean you should not present it in the best light possible. Here are some common reasons for leaving and the ways you can interpret them more positively.

I was heartily bored	I was offered a more challenging job (in management / that would make use of my skills in marketing, etc)
I had to move house	Unavoidable circumstances forced a move from my former home, but I am now settled in this area
I was stuck without a chance of promotion	I felt my skills and experience would have more scope in a larger organization
I was sacked	The company I worked for made staff changes due to a reorganiza-tion (if applicable. After all, there is more than one way of being sacked)

You may have to give reasons for leaving every job you mention on your form, so make sure they are not all the same. For some reason variety is more believable.

It should perhaps be said that you should never, under any circumstances, say anything bad about a previous employer. This will only indicate that you may be a potential source of trouble, or that you are lazy and intractable and lacking in self-confidence. You will not be offered the position.

Other work-related questions

Other questions sometimes encountered in this section of the form include:

'Do you require notice before references are requested?'

Always tick 'No' here. If you tick 'Yes', what does that say about you? That you have not been sufficiently organized to notify your referees that they are, in fact, your referees? That you want to make a last, panicky phone call to get them on side? That you are hoping the employer will never ask you for the references and they'll just give you the job? That your references are fictional?

There's no escape. Tick 'No'. Otherwise, at the very best, you are just making more work for your potential employers, and how do you think that will make them feel?

> *'Can we contact your present employer?'*

Tick 'Yes'. See above.

> *'Are you related to anyone in the company/organization?'*

Be truthful. This hardly seems worth lying about anyway, and even if you were to get away with it, if it were discovered later it could be grounds for dismissal.

> *'What is your previous supervisor's name/phone number?'*

Give it. No omissions. But make sure you tell the supervisor.

> *'What period of notice do you require from your current employment?'*

Make it as short as you can.

Covering statement

The covering statement is, with reason, the most feared section. But, with some systematic thought, it can be turned to your advantage. This is the point where you can really outdistance the other candidates, in the cogency, detail, relevance and impact of your response.

The section can be titled 'Additional information' or 'Explain why you are a suitable candidate for this post' or 'How do your skills and experience relate to the post for which you have applied?' It is the same thing: it is a way for the recruiter to find the stronger candidates.

What should you do to prepare this section, then?

1. Look hard at the job specification and person specification. This will be detailed in the original advertisement, or in supplementary information sent with the application form, or both. Take each point and write notes matching each point, then build your covering statement to match the whole exactly. Do not omit any. If you leave out any aspect of the requirements you will immediately rank lower in the screening process, and it may lose you the chance of an interview.

2. Break the covering statement into sections, with a heading for each of the specifications that you are addressing and any additional ones. This makes it easier to read. It also makes it easier for the recruiter to see that you are methodical, and that you have covered all the bases.

3. In the person specification, there may be elements marked 'essential' and 'preferred'. What the recruiter is saying is that the ideal candidate will have both, but that in the absence of any candidates who have both, candidates who have only the essential skills may be considered (as long as the rest of the application is up to scratch). The unavoidable conclusion is this: unless you are sure that none of the candidates will have all the essential and preferred qualities – an unlikely proposition in a competitive job market – it would be unwise not to address all the criteria, both essential and preferred, in the covering statement. If you do not address them all, the person who does will get the job. This leads us on to the next point.

4. Use transferable skills to cover all the bases if you are missing something. If you really do not have the experience they are asking for then do not apply. It will be a waste of your time and theirs. If, on the other hand, you have other skills and achievements which are not strictly relevant but a good case could be made for them being transferable, then do so. For example, the person specification for a job as a librarian might call for someone who has excellent customer service skills. You may never have worked directly with the public, but did once have a job teaching English at a summer school. In that position, you had to assess and respond to students' needs in a friendly and relaxed manner, research queries, and build relationships with the many different staff and pupils. Right there you have the transferable skills needed for work in customer service. If, however, you left that base uncovered in your application, you would be much less likely to be considered for interview.

5. Think about the personality of the person they are looking for, and try to project yourself as that person. This will help you, especially if you feel you are somewhat lacking in direct experience of the particular field involved. For example, think about the type of personality needed to staff a display stand at a trade

exhibition. Then think about the personality needed to take a small party of tourists around a popular resort. In both cases you would need to be extrovert, articulate, friendly, well-organized, confident and quick-witted, with a sense of humour. The two jobs have many things in common, but the nature of the two types of business is completely different. Knowledge of products or experience in a particular field isn't always of paramount importance. Having the right personality can sometimes top both.

6. If you have skills or experience in an unofficial or unpaid capacity, mention them. For example, if you are applying for a position as a supervisor but have no previous experience, mention that when working in retail you had many opportunities to train junior staff, helped to run a sales campaign in which you were in charge of a small team of people in-store, and so on. The same applies for voluntary work or even college projects. If it has any relevance, mention it to avoid leaving gaps.

7. Job advertisements often say 'training will be given', but if you can demonstrate some relevant experience, you will beat other candidates who do not. So if you already have some experience, make it known.

8. Research the company and get to know its raison d'être. Use any examples of mission statements or commitments found on its website or in brochures. If the company is committed to environmentalism, you must be too.

9. Use concrete examples. Actual examples are always the most powerful statements. As in the CV, you need to concentrate on things done and achieved. You should always analyze these in terms of benefits to the employer, asking yourself: how much money did I save? How much time? What new efficiencies were introduced?

10. Use of figures will be important here. It is much more effective to say, for example,

> *Increased sales by 50% year-on-year, enabling the department to expand from five to nine full-time staff in three years.*

than

> *Helped to improve sales and oversaw staff recruitment.*

Statistics are oddly comforting. We all know that they can be misleading, but we respond to them because we think that here is something that can be verified. If it is a lie, at least there's a chance to catch the perpetrator out, whereas if it were just a piece of windy self-promotion we'd ultimately be none the wiser.

11. Focus on value for the employer. It will very probably be true that you want this job for what you can get out of it: money, status, fulfilment, social contact. It may seem odd, but you should not give any of these primary concerns as explanations of why you are applying for the post. What you must focus on instead is the contribution you can make, the value-for-money that you can give, the hard work that you will be willing to put in, the efficiency with which you can do that work. You must show that you can save them money.

12. Round it off. Give something extra as well as the essential matching of all the job requirements. Use the details of your CV career objective to show what a focused and determined person you are and underline your commitment to giving value to the employer. You might say something like this:

> *In summary: I am a friendly and hardworking person with an excellent grasp of the new technologies relevant to this*

post. I am enthusiastic about computers and would be willing to give all my energies to smooth and successful database management. I would very much welcome an opportunity to demonstrate my aptitude at an interview.

Covering statement practicalities

Lastly, some practical things for you to consider:

- If you prefer to type this section, you do not necessarily need to use the page provided to do it on – this can lead to problems with spacing, and you may mistakenly print over part of the question. It is perfectly acceptable to write 'see attached' and then to type on a separate sheet, labelling the attachment clearly with the title of the section it refers to. Put your name and address on each additional sheet.

- You will often find that another part of the form asks you to give your reasons for applying for the post. If you think about it, this is slightly different from your suitability, so try to keep the two sections distinct from one another, avoiding repetition of information. Repetition will be perceived as carelessness (see page 63).

Referees

Application forms almost always ask for referees, but the truth is that references are almost never taken up until after an offer of employment has been made. It is too time-consuming for recruiters to look at the references of all the candidates. Employers know that references are always going to be good. If they weren't, the candidates wouldn't have selected those particular people. That's why it is superfluous to include the names on your CV.

However, as the situation stands, you will probably have to include referees on your form. It may stipulate who they may or may not be: for example it may say that neither may be related to you and that one should be your most recent employer or tutor. When giving referees' names, as already mentioned in the CV section, do not forget to do one important thing: tell them about it. If they do not know they are your referees and have half-forgotten about you, you have sown the seeds for a disaster when the human resources department rings them up. Remind your referees of your existence and bring them up to speed on what you are doing and where you are trying to get to, and then, when the time comes, they will be much more useful.

Other common questions

All forms differ. Here are some of the other common questions or requests that you might encounter:

'What are your reasons for applying for this post?'

This is probably the most common of the 'wild-card' questions you might come across. As mentioned above, this is rather different to the question of why you feel you are suitable for the post (the subject of your 'covering statement'). It is instead ostensibly about what you feel you could get out of it. It would be easy to say here 'I want a more exciting career,' 'I am looking for a better salary,' 'My previous employment was not stimulating enough,' 'I would like a more senior position.' Do not fall into this trap. You still need to make this section about them, not about you. If you wrote any of the things above, they might think you were an awkward customer, a restless excitement-seeker or an egomaniac. Employers do not know you for the lovable person you are: they have to assume the worst. Here are some ways you can start off sentences which put things more delicately but still fall into the area of 'reasons for applying':

- I think I could make a contribution …
- I think I have the personality skills appropriate for this kind of work …
- I am looking for opportunities for rewarding work in which I can demonstrate the skills that have in the past made me a valuable employee …
- I wish to move into a position where I can demonstrate my ability to …
- I think I share some of the company's goals to provide …

OTHER COMMON QUESTIONS

- Your company is working in an exciting field in which I feel I can make a positive impact ...
- I feel that my recent experience makes me particularly qualified for this job ...
- I think I would enjoy the challenges of the post ...
- I feel I can bring a great deal of energy and enthusiasm to the post ...
- I enjoy leading and motivating others ...

'How would you ensure equal opportunities in this post?'

This is an interesting question. It relates mainly to the employer's concerns that they might not be doing enough to fulfil their obligations under equal opportunity legislation relating to sex, race, sexuality, age and so on, and their ensuing desire to hire people who are like-minded. You will be much more likely to find it where you are applying for a post in some kind of community health/relations field, and less likely to find it if you are applying for work as a portfolio manager.

The strategy that will probably work best here is to give a brief example of how you have confronted discrimination in the past. Think about any case where either you have been personally affected, or you have met people who have had particular experiences of discrimination, or heard them talk about the issues they have felt to be important. You might also like to underline the fact that you are aware of (and support) standard anti-discrimination policies in the workplace, and are familiar with the relevant legislation (see page 70). You may also wish to quote from legislation relating to particular institutions. For example, the Special Educational Needs and Disability Act requires that universities and colleges make 'reasonable adjustments' to their facilities to provide for disabled students where they would otherwise be at a 'substantial disadvantage'. The Act requires that these bodies 'anticipate' rather than 'react to' the needs of disabled students. If you can quote from the right rule-book it will be impressive. (Tip:

look the legislation up on the web.)

'What attracts you to this organization?'

Do some research. Look at the company's promotional materials and their website. Without concrete detail your answers will not look very impressive. Aim for something that shows insider knowledge. If applying for a position at a wind farm, say something like 'I believe the future of Britain's energy supply lies in wind power, and from my research into your new generation of direct drive, variable speed turbines, I feel that UK Wind Systems will be the company that leads this energy revolution.'

'What do you consider are the strengths of your personality?'

This is perhaps difficult for British people. Modesty is still considered a virtue, and bragging about one's achievements and personal qualities in rather poor taste. If you think this is an outdated perception, think how your friends would answer a verbal question about their strengths. If they admitted to any at all, it would probably be in a form such as 'I'm quite creative,' or 'I think I'm sometimes rather good at managing people.' The qualifiers 'quite', 'I think' 'sometimes' and 'rather' are very much part of the way British people express themselves, and this self-deprecation can carry over into the way they write. The application form is not the place for bashfulness, however. It requires assertiveness and salesmanship. What's needed in the answer to the above question is something like:

Creative innovation	At Barley Stores I successfully turned around three underperforming outlets with targeted refits and product promotions.
Good at managing people	I have developed strong interpersonal skills in a career dealing with staff at all levels.

If, as in the first point above, you can provide examples of ways in which you have demonstrated these personality traits, so much the better.

If you experience difficulty in listing your good points, try asking someone who knows you well. They might be surprised to be asked at first but will probably enjoy helping you assess your personality. They may also be able to give you examples of the ways you have exhibited these strengths, which you can then use in your application.

> *'What are your interests outside work, and what have you gained from them?'*

As mentioned in the CV section, make your interests ... interesting. Do not mention TV or cooking. They are boring, unless you are a *Masterchef* entrant.

You can profitably mention most sports, since they often indicate team-playing skills, ability to delegate/lead, determination, self-motivation and analytical ability (see page 43 in the 'CVs' section).

Other categories of things worth mentioning include awards or distinctions, language skills attained (see page 44; there may be a separate box for this), and anything where you have won the endorsement of your peers by being appointed or elected to a position.

Voluntary work is crucial here, although you may already have mentioned it elsewhere, for example in the 'breaks from employment' section or the 'covering statement' section. If you have ever done any voluntary work, do not leave it out – put it somewhere. It makes a powerful statement that you are willing to help others, keen to get involved in your community, and not lazy, selfish or cynical.

What have you gained from any of the above? This is a golden opportunity. Some of the things that may be gained from personal interests are the ability to work productively with others; an understanding of the value of determination; a sense of responsibility for others; the ability to work under pressure; the conquest of fears of public speaking; an awareness of the needs of people with disabilities; or a hundred other skills and achievements. Do not waste this further opportunity to sell yourself.

'Do you have any criminal convictions, spent or otherwise?'

The Rehabilitation of Offenders Act (1974) makes provision for people who have had criminal convictions but have paid their debt to society. Once a certain period of time has elapsed (which varies according to the seriousness of the crime) the offence is described as 'spent' and need not be declared. However, there are some jobs in which a conviction can never be classed as spent. These are notably jobs to do with providing social and community services or working with children. In these cases all convictions, however long ago, must be declared.

The employer has a duty to make it clear on the form or accompanying information whether you are required to declare spent convictions for that particular post. If it simply says 'Have you ever been convicted of a criminal offence?', and does not, either there or in the accompanying information, say that spent convictions must also be declared, you do not need to declare them.

If you do have a criminal conviction that requires declaration, it will not necessarily debar you from the post, but, depending somewhat on the seriousness of the offence, the unfortunate reality is that it is highly unlikely you will be granted an interview. This is presumably the purpose of the aforesaid Act: to make declaration non-compulsory so that former offenders are allowed to get on with their lives and fulfil their potential.

OTHER COMMON QUESTIONS

'Do you have a full clean driving licence?'

A standard question for jobs that involve any driving. If you have points on your licence, mention them; as long as they are not approaching the statutory limit this is unlikely to debar you from consideration for an interview.

> *'How many days' absence from work have you had in the last 12 months due to illness?'*

If you have had a lot of time off sick in the last twelve months, you have some explaining to do. Employers are very wary of candidates who have a bad record in this area. The only advice, if you have had, say, a month off, is to compare the previous year with the three years before that, in which you had (let's say) an average of two days off per annum. You can then say something such as: 'Last November I contracted pleurisy and was forced to take a month off work to recuperate; I am pleased to say I have now made a full recovery and my doctor informs me it is unlikely to recur. In the previous three years I had an average of only two days every year off from work, the lowest in my department, and I fully expect this to be the pattern in future.' If your record goes above around seven to ten days for the last twelve months, and you are fairly sure that your current employer will be asked about this, it is wise to include some sort of explanation, which also gives you an opportunity to state that your health is now excellent (if it is).

Declaration

The final part of any form is the declaration. Have a look back through the form, reviewing it for accuracy and truthfulness, but also checking whether it is everything it could be in terms of impact and salesmanship. Then, if you have not already done so, read the terms and conditions of the application, which should be included somewhere in the accompanying material. This is actually of some importance, since it may commit you to some things that might surprise you, including:

- working overtime
- maintaining your driving licence on pain of dismissal
- drug screening
- medical checks
- physical demonstration of job-related skills
- instant dismissal without giving a reason within a given probation time
- agreeing to all or any checks on your public records, including credit history, criminal and motor vehicle records

Your rights at this point are rather fewer in number but still important:

- You have the right to data protection.
- You have the right not to be discriminated against.
- You have the right to withhold unspent convictions unless otherwise stated.

If you are happy with that, sign it. You have finished.

Part Three

Covering Letters

A personal communication

Your CV is word-perfect. It is a highly persuasive document that sells your skills and achievements. But maybe the rest of your application is not. Then all your efforts will have gone to waste.

CVs have traditionally been accompanied by letters. Even advertisers who say simply 'Send your CV ...' expect a letter to arrive as well. Employers like the personal touch that a letter provides.

And from the candidate's point of view, the covering letter is also an important part of the application. It acts as the intermediary: the salesperson for your CV. Written well, it makes people want to read more. It can make the difference between a noticed CV and a wasted CV.

So how should you write one? There are many things you can do to produce a good covering letter, and in this section you will find all the essential tips and tricks. But it is helpful to bear in mind one idea above all: in writing it, you should try to project yourself as the sort of person the recipient would want to employ. The key word here is 'person'. The covering letter is a personal communication, unlike a CV or an application form. It is addressed to a named person and is signed by a named person. It has the sense of an attempt to establish a relationship and will be much more of an indicator to the reader of personality than the CV or application form. And as such, it will be their way of judging whether that person will fit into the company.

Employers want to see what candidates can offer and personal qualities, as evidenced in the letter, will be crucial to their decision. Among the many qualities that your letter can signal are politeness, confidence, enthusiasm, sensitivity, assertiveness, consideration, seriousness, reliability, flexibility and flair. Of course, if you are not careful you might also signal flashiness, pretentiousness, rudeness, desperation, aggressiveness and egotism. All these things can appear in the covering letter.

Structure

The 'three-act structure' is a technique for moving a story along in three main sections – in more familiar terms, a beginning, a middle and an end. Similarly, when it comes to the structure of a covering letter, what are required are paragraphs: an opening paragraph, a middle paragraph, and a closing paragraph, with each paragraph expressing a single main idea. You will see from this that an ideal covering letter should not be more than one page long. Its function is not to reproduce what is in the CV. Its function is to stimulate interest by telling a brief, pertinent story.

Opening paragraph: grab their interest

The main purpose of the opening paragraph is to explain why you are writing. For the job, of course, but you can also say where you saw the advertisement (if there was one), when it was published (if it was) and what your particular reason is for being interested in the company. It will often go something like this:

> *I am writing in response to your advertisement for a lathe operator in the Braydon Evening Post of the 2nd January. The job reference number is 1087A.*

This is a simple opening paragraph of two sentences and does the job. It is an excellent beginning for someone who wants to project themselves as steady and reliable. However, imagine you are applying for a post that requires a little showmanship and person-ality; you might want to start the letter rather differently. A sales representative, who needs to be friendly and persuasive, might try the following:

I have always respected PPP Marketing as an industry leader, so I was excited to see evidence of your latest recruitment drive.

Another method is to see how the company presents itself in its promotional materials. Look at its website and its brochures. See how it presents its unique selling point, then match your unique selling point to it. For example, you may be looking for work as an estate agent and you notice that the local company has been experimenting with their board designs to suggest a more youthful, unconventional image. If you project yourself to fit in with that image you are more likely to be successful, as in the following:

Having worked as an estate agent for four years, I have always felt attracted to your company. Your way of dealing with the public manages to be efficient without seeming stuffy, and fun without being frivolous. I feel I could offer a company like yours a high level of dedication and drive.

Alternatively you could lead off with a piece of technical information that shows your knowledge of the market:

From my research into convention sales I have noticed that the name of ZZ Promotions is a universally respected provider in the field. The recent decision of TrustLodge to adopt ZZ as its Favoured Partner speaks volumes about ZZ's growing market share, and I believe I could make a positive contribution to such an innovative company.

If you find during your job-search that you are not getting any results, it may be that the opening of your covering letter is simply not strong enough. For example, if you are working in a fairly traditional field such as law, you are probably sending out fairly traditional covering letters. The problem is that all the law firms will be receiving a steady influx of similar covering letters. Why not try changing this:

> *I note that on the 12th inst you advertised for a legal junior ...*

to this?

> *I thought I would write and introduce myself. Your company is already very well known to me.*

It is slightly startling, yet not disrespectful, and may well produce much more of a response.

One common situation is when you are writing a covering letter as a follow-up to a recent phone conversation. Often you phone for an application form or other information and during the process speak to someone who might later make a decision about your application. This is a godsend, so don't waste it. If you start off:

> *I am writing in response to our telephone conversation of Monday the 15th. As you will see from the enclosed CV, I have a successful track record ...*

you will effectively nullify any potential influence of that personal contact. Try an opening like this instead:

> *Thank you for taking the time to talk to me last Monday. I enjoyed our conversation, especially hearing about the reasons behind your current reorganization. I didn't know Swindon was such a hive of activity. You were kind enough to ask me to send you a follow-up letter detailing my skills and achievements, so here it is ...*

This sounds more personal, and allows you to establish yourself as a particular human being rather than a piece of paper or a computer file. Anything that distinguishes you in this way is extremely important to your chances of success.

Middle paragraph: set out your stall

The middle paragraph is the place where you set out a chosen few of your skills and achievements. Don't regard this as an opportunity to simply cut and paste information from your CV, as being forced to read the same information twice will not be appreciated.

The best strategy is to go back to the original advertisement. There you will probably encounter two main sections: the job specification and the person specification (see the section beginning on page 65). The person specification will often be divided into two: what is essential and what is preferred. Take these as the starting point for your middle paragraph. You may wish to use bulleted points:

> *I was particularly interested to see your advertisement, since it matched my skills and achievements with great accuracy. I have:*
>
> - *Ten years' experience in the automotive industry*
> - *Expertise with DFT paint application*
> - *Experience in refitting shops in line with the 2004 guidelines*
>
> *In addition I am:*
>
> - *Hardworking and reliable*
> - *A flexible shift-worker*
> - *A fast learner with a range of computer skills*

If you put this as continuous prose, changing some of the verbs and splitting the middle paragraph into two for readability, you might come up with something such as:

I was particularly interested to see your advertisement, since it matched my skills and achievements with great accuracy. I am an experienced factory floor operative with ten years in the automotive industry. I have wide experience of DFT paint application, and more recently I have refitted shops in line with the 2004 DTI guidelines.

In addition, I am hardworking and reliable, a flexible shift-worker of many years' standing and a fast learner with a range of computer skills.

This addresses what the employer wants. If possible you can go one step further by offering something unique that fewer of the other candidates will have. It could be some kind of award or record, perhaps a time-keeping record:

You may also be interested to note that in the last ten years I have only missed an average of one day of work per annum through illness, which, while I worked for GG Motors, was the best attendance record across the entire staff.

The middle paragraph should not be tentative or humble; it should be bold and confident. Achievements expressed using the '-ed' forms of verbs will often sound the most respectfully assertive. Phrases such as 'I think' or 'I feel' are best omitted, because they imply that the achievements listed are a matter of opinion and not of fact.

Perhaps the main rule of the middle paragraph is that you should always keep your employer in mind. Your skills and achievements are not there for you to boast about yourself but to address what you can do to help them with their staffing problems. As a consequence you should not begin every sentence with 'I' or 'My':

> ✗ *I recently saw your advertisement ... I think the position would suit my career path perfectly ... I am looking for more challenging work ... I wish to increase the chance of promotion ... I would like to expand my management experience ... I would welcome the opportunity to work with you ... My CV is enclosed ...*

Instead, try to break this up with the judicious use of other beginnings. You can even begin, in some cases, with 'You', 'Your company' and so on:

> ✔ *You will notice that my CV matches your requirements perfectly ... Market share has been a dominant concern of my working life as an Account Manager ... Your company is widely known for its creative innovation, and I feel I could contribute ... The nature of the industry demands people who can ...*

This sort of strategy is far more likely to leave them thinking that you have their needs in mind.

Closing paragraph: get them to talk to you

The main idea of the closing paragraph should be this: I would like to meet you. To express this idea, you can ask for one of two things, or possibly both: that they contact you or that they grant you the permission to contact them. Here are some examples:

> *From my own experience as a manager I know that CVs are generally useful to establish the outstanding candidates, but that only an interview can find the candidate who is exactly right. To demonstrate that I am that candidate I would welcome the chance of a personal meeting.*

If you would like to meet to discuss how my skills and experience could benefit your company in the future, I would be very happy to hear from you.

I would welcome the chance of a personal meeting if you think I could be of some assistance in this area.

My CV is attached. If you would like to discuss how I may be of help to you in your current projects I would be very glad to come in and meet you.

I know that your time is valuable, but if you were to call me on 01222 334455, I am positive that you would feel it was time well spent.

If you would like me to expand on any of the material contained in my CV I would be delighted to come in and meet you sometime. I am available on 01234 67589.

You will notice, again, that the needs of the employer are paramount here.

Ask for it?

All of the closing paragraphs above ask for the employer to contact the candidate. It is, however, possible for the candidate to announce the intention, ever so politely, of contacting the employer. This will probably depend to a certain extent on the kind of work being applied for. Jobs differ and people differ. If you are applying for work in sales, a go-getter is admired and understood.

Still, do tone it down as much as possible. The language should be qualified, since you are asking for something rather than stating something. Don't say 'I will call you', whatever you might read in self-help manuals. This sounds over-assertive to British ears. Try instead 'May I take the liberty of calling you sometime next week on this matter?' or 'Perhaps I might contact you?'

> *As you will see from my enclosed CV, I have the skills and experience that are essential for this fast-paced industry. I am sure that a personal meeting would establish that beyond doubt. May I call you to arrange an interview?*

> *I would very much like to meet you and discuss what I can do to help PPX Incorporated grow into its true place in the Industrial Cleaning market. May I take the liberty of calling you next week to arrange an interview? I am sure that we would both find this a positive experience.*

Finally, end with a 'thank you', on its own line. Then on the final line, put 'Yours sincerely', followed by a space, then your signature, then your name:

> *I hope you agree after looking at my CV that I have a great deal to contribute in this area. If I may, I will call you next week; alternatively, please feel free to contact me at your convenience.*

> *Thank you,*

> *Yours sincerely,*

> *Rachel Easton*

> *Rachel Easton*

Why 'Yours sincerely'? Because you are always going to be addressing it to a named person, of which more in the next section.

Finding the right person

The most disastrous way to begin a covering letter is to write 'Dear Sir/Madam'. It shows that you have not made even the most basic effort to find out who is likely to be dealing with your application.

We can narrow down the options that you might be faced with when trying to find an addressee. They are:

- You are responding to an advertisement in which the correct addressee is named.
- You are responding to an advertisement in which the correct addressee is not named.
- You are writing a cold letter and don't know the addressee.

In the first option, your task has been done for you. In the second, no one is specified, so ring the company and ask them, or look it up on their website.

In the third option, when you are writing cold letters, who should you address them to: human resources or management? The answer in most cases is management. They are the people who will ultimately make the decision. It is sometimes thought that management do not actually recruit. This is a mistake.

How do you find which decision-maker is the right one? You can phone, consult directories, or, most convenient of all, use the company website which is more likely to be updated regularly. If you use a trade publication such as *The Riveting Yearbook* the information could be out of date.

FINDING THE RIGHT PERSON

The yearbook is still useful in one respect though: the telephone numbers will probably still be current. You can then ring them up and ask for the name of the head of Rivet Supply (Eastern Division). Very occasionally switchboards are reluctant to give out this information, for example when certain departments get a very high volume of unsolicited mail. It helps to give them a gentle prompt and say 'I'm just calling to ask whether Jim Sterne is still head of Rivet Supply.' They are more likely to respond to an approach such as this.

If you are trying to find the e-mail addresses of members of staff, it is sometimes even more difficult to get the information on the phone. However, there is a trade secret. When companies give out e-mail addresses, especially large companies, they usually do so on a pre-formatted basis. Firstname.lastname@company.com is a common one. Firstininital.lastname@company.com is another, and firstinitial_lastname@company.com yet another. As long as you can find one company e-mail address (there is certain to be one on the website, even if it is only customer services) and you know the name of the person you want to speak to, you can often deduce the address you want. Sometimes, switchboard operators who will not give particular e-mail addresses, will give the magic formula, especially if you prompt them. You can casually ask them: 'Could you just confirm for me, is the company e-mail address in the form "firstname.lastname@company.com"?' It rarely fails.

It used to be standard advice always to write the covering letter, but unless there is a specific request that it be handwritten, this is no longer advised. A typewritten covering letter with a handwritten signature and perhaps a letterhead looks much more professional. Handwritten covering letters are now very unusual, so if you write one you will be very unusual too, and there are some areas in which it is unwise to stand out too much. Covering letters should be written on-screen using a word-processing package rather than typed on a typewriter, if possible. This shows familiarity with computers.

A typed covering letter is likely to be more convenient for the applicant as well as more acceptable to the employer. If it is stored as a file on your computer (or several files, if you wish to vary the style), then you will not have to write it out by hand each time.

Letterheads are a good device for standing out from the crowd, and are extremely easy to create. You don't need to create a logo, of course; you are a person, not an organization. Computer software now offers an almost unlimited range of fonts and colours, so you can arrive very quickly and easily at something like this:

> 123 Broad Street
> Slough
> SL19 2RT
> Tel: 01234 567890
> Mobile: 077 777 5567
>
> E-mail f.smith@anyserver.com
> Web: www.f-smith.com

PRESENTATION

It does not matter if the typeface is slightly larger for the letter-head. If you use, say, a 10-point face in the text, your letterhead can easily be 12 point.

The type of paper you use is also important. If you can, use a weight and style of paper similar to that on which your CV is printed. Make the paper heavy without being regal; 100–120 gsm is fine. As far as fonts go, use a standard one such as Arial, Verdana or Times New Roman, at a point size of 10 or 12.

Much of what has already been said on the subject of spelling and grammar need not be repeated here (see page 63); all that needs to be stressed is that it must be correct. Ensure names and dates are correct. Make a rough draft first, and if you make a mistake in the final printed version, do not add correction fluid or handwritten corrections as this looks messy and unprofessional. Ask someone else to read it and check for any mistakes if you are not sure.

Cold letters

The singer Madonna once said: 'Most people don't get what they want because they don't ask for it.' This is true in many areas of life, but especially in looking for work. Applying for advertised positions, where they have effectively asked you to respond, is fine but it may not be enough to get you a job. You may need to ask them before you are successful.

Some of the opening gambits you can adopt for cold letters have been explored on pages 97–9. A standard cold letter will begin something like this:

> *I wish to enquire about any vacancy you may have in your Sales Department. Your customer services manager, Don Griffiths, suggested I write to you.*

But you can easily ring the changes and write something like this:

> *Conventional wisdom is that Journalism and Marketing don't have much in common. As someone who has experience in both fields I would beg to disagree. My experience of both makes me well placed to help in your South-east Asian marketing drive. Let me explain …*

Cold letters can be made considerably less cold by reference to some sort of named contact. If you have heard about the vacancy from someone, mention who they are:

> *Eric Johnson of TTFN Productions suggested I write to you to outline how I could be of assistance in your current project.*

Try also, as a more urgent priority than in a conventional response to an advertisement, to demonstrate knowledge of the company and any inside information, showing that you have made an informed decision in applying to them:

> *The recent news that M&G is to merge with D&J is an exciting new development; I believe I could make a positive contribution as an account manager in such a forward-looking company.*

Another useful strategy is to actively anticipate the employer's needs. Try thinking about where the company is going. This will take a lot of research, but it could pay off handsomely. Consider the following approach:

> *From my research into your recent expansion into the Midlands I note that you have just completed a major new distribution centre at Conglebridge. As an experienced warehouse manager, may I offer my services at this important time?*

Let's have a look at some real examples. The two letters here are targeted at two different situations: firstly, a response to an advertised position, and secondly, a cold or unsolicited letter. Before you read them, here's a brief checklist of the do's and don'ts already mentioned:

Do
- Limit it to one page
- Use three main paragraphs
- Address it to a person
- Say where you saw the advertisement (if applicable)
- Interest the employer with selected skills and achievements
- Include information which betrays your research/knowledge of the company
- Tell them why they need you
- Refer them to the CV
- Do their thinking for them

Don't
- Address it to a 'Dear Sir/Madam'
- End 'Yours faithfully'
- Be too pushy in saying that you will contact them
- Outline the benefits you expect for yourself
- Use qualified language such as may/might/I think/ I believe/quite, except when requesting their permission for you to contact them
- Write the same letter for each vacancy
- Use off-the-peg phrases such as 'I enjoy challenging work'

123 Broad Street
Slough
SL19 2RT
Tel: 01234 567890
Mobile: 077 777 5567

E-mail f.smith@anyserver.com
Web: www.f-smith.com

Mr D Smithwick
Chief Analyst
DDD Investments
Threadneedle St
London W1 4RT

19 May 2006

Dear Mr Smithwick

I would like to apply for the position of Financial Analyst as advertised in
The Guardian of 14 May, job reference number 5566.

As you will see from my CV, I am particularly qualified for this post. I have:

• Nine years' experience as a financial analyst and consultant
• Extensive experience of the Frankfurt market
• Thorough understanding of the relevant software systems
• Excellent verbal and written communication skills in English and German

If you would like to meet to discuss how my skills and experience could
benefit your company in the future, I would be very happy to hear from you.

Thank you.

Yours sincerely

Francine Smith

Francine Smith

1. Covering letter for an advertised position

123 Broad Street
Slough
SL19 2RT
Tel: 01234 567890
Mobile: 077 777 5567
E-mail f.smith@anyserver.com
Web: www.f-smith.com

Alexandra Maxwell
Senior Manager
HT Indexing
24-28 Finchley Rd
London N12 3RT

13 December 2006

Dear Ms Maxwell

From my research into the Machine Indexing sector I have noticed that the name of HT is a universally respected provider in the field. I believe I could make a positive contribution to such an innovative company.

My skills and experience cover machine maintenance and refitting; CAD-CAM applications; MRT operations; and the control and successful reduction of operating costs in a competitive environment. As a shop floor manager of 7 years' standing I have managed teams of up to 15 staff. I am a hardworking, flexible self-starter.

You may also be interested to note that I have taken an average of one day off work per annum through illness in the last ten years, which, while I worked for GG Motors, was the best attendance record across the entire staff.

I hope you agree after looking at my CV that I have a great deal to contribute in this area. If I may, I will call you next week; alternatively, please feel free to contact me at your convenience.

Thank you.

Yours sincerely

Frederick Smith

Frederick Smith

2. Cold letter

There is another approach to the covering letter that takes these principles and boils them down even further. It is known as the job brief (or employment briefing, or executive summary). It is being seen increasingly in the job market, and is based on the idea that human resources or personnel departments, rather than managers, are often the first point of contact for covering letters.

The needs of human resources departments are often fairly basic. They are usually only there as screeners, and may not (in the initial stages) know much about the day-to-day requirements of the post, so the idea of a persuasive 'sell' may be somewhat beside the point. The job brief allows the human resources department manager to see immediately that here is a candidate who fulfils the requirements of the advertisement. An example is given on the following page.

You will note this is not addressed to anyone. However, its sharp focus and brevity make it quite compelling. If you are only addressing a human resources department and are responding to an advertised position, this could be a method worth trying.

Job Brief for the position of Supermarket Manager, as advertised in the *Eastern Daily News*, 20.6.2006

Elaine McLeish
123 The Street
Manchester M60 5TY
E-mail e.mcleish@anyserver.com
Tel: 01234 56789

With your selection procedures in mind I have composed the job brief below. In the left column are the specifications of the post as advertised, and on the right the ways in which my skills and experience match those specifications. I hope this is useful in saving you time. My CV is also attached.

Position applied for: Supermarket Manager	Current position: Supermarket Supervisor
Advertised requirements:	Relevant skills and experience:
Four years or more in supermarket management	Six years' experience running a busy supermarket butchery department
Creative leadership skills	Supervised a team of 20; praised for innovative approach
Flair for presentation and display	Redesigned large department, including floor layout, display, lighting and back room
Focus on the speciality and organics market	Commitment to organics
Excellent interpersonal skills	Known for ability to motivate workforce
Interest in sustainable farming	Experience and interest in sourcing free-range meat

E-mailing covering letters

Job advertisements will often say 'E-mail your CV to ...' and give an address (see page 51 for details of how to send and attach your CV). It will still be advantageous to write a covering letter to accompany it. As mentioned above, covering letters, unlike CVs, are personal communications. If you miss out on this personal contact you are wasting an opportunity and every chance counts.

The principles of e-mail covering letters are essentially the same as those of ordinary covering letters:

- Address it to a real person.
- Be brief and to the point.
- Say which job you are applying for and where you saw the advertisement.
- Interest the employer with selected skills and achievements.
- Include information which illustrates your knowledge of the company.
- Don't outline the benefits to yourself, but do outline the benefits to them.
- Don't use qualified language.

However, there are some aspects of an e-mail covering letter that are different. For example, it would seem rather odd to reproduce all the heading information in an e-mail that one generally finds at the top of a printed letter, such as the addresses (yours and theirs), and contact details. Your address and contacts should be left to the end of the e-mail and go beneath the signature. Give your phone number in this final block of information, but not your e-mail address as they will already have that through you e-mailing them. Another difference is that e-mails are more informal. This often manifests itself in letters that begin 'Hi ...' or 'Hello ...' rather than 'Dear ...'. However, in the initial stages of your job application at least, this should be avoided. Begin 'Dear ...' and address it to a named person.

In the body of the e-mail try aiming for a balance between informality and professionalism. E-mails will often be briefer than printed letters, with less reliance on the more orotund manner of writing that produces phrases such as 'I remain available for interview at your convenience.' Try instead 'Please feel free to give me a call.' For your very last line you might prefer to try something less formal than 'Yours sincerely', and put instead 'Regards' or 'Best regards'. 'Yours faithfully' is definitely out.

Finally, the world of electronic mail is dogged by a persistent disdain for the laws of spelling and grammar. People often leave errors uncorrected, even though they know they are there. You are strongly advised not to succumb. Poor spelling, and mistakes of grammar and punctuation, will still count against you.

Trying to find work involves many different skills. One of the most important is effective administration. You will very probably start to accumulate lots of pieces of paper and computer files. You will need to organize them properly so that you feel in control of the process. If you feel sure that your job-search is proceeding along orderly lines you will be able to act with much more confidence.

Applying for more than one job at once

Most people will need to apply for more than one job before they are successful. Rejection is a part of the process, not an indication that you are unemployable. It may even be healthy. Not getting the job could easily signal that you would not have been happy had you got it.

But, given that you will probably have to make multiple applications, what is the correct procedure? Consecutive or simultaneous applications? The answer is 'simultaneous': apply for more than one job at the same time. It is not unethical. If you post off one application form and wait a month before hearing that you have been 'unsuccessful on this occasion', you have just wasted that month.

The only problem you will come across if you make simultaneous applications is that you may receive more than one interview offer. This is what the Japanese refer to as a 'luxury problem' – a delicious dilemma for people who do not have any real problems.

Having said that, be cautious as to how many you start off with. Test the waters with a small batch first and see how many interview offers, if any, it pulls in. This will enable you to judge the size of your next batch, which may have to be larger.

Job record

You are probably going to have a lot of applications on the boil. The best thing to do to prevent the process getting out of control is to create a document, either on your computer or on paper – or on a huge board that dominates your living room – that you can add to and refer to. It might look something like this:

Company	Job title	Closing date	Application sent	E-mail/ snail mail	Should hear by	Result
Integrated Fruit Juice	Manager	12.7.06	8.7.06	e-mail	24.7.06	
Mr Juice	Buyer	30.7.06				
Penfold's Organic	Product Developer	not specified	14.7.06	snail mail	?5.8.06	

By having a column for 'closing date' you can use this table to list jobs you need to apply for soon as well as ones you have already applied for.

The 'should hear by' column allows you to review the progress of each application and chase it up individually if necessary. Some employers will let you know, whether informally over the telephone, or formally in a letter of receipt for your application, when a decision will be made (the 'should hear by' date). If you haven't been given one, though, enter a date three weeks after mailing or e-mailing your application.

You will perhaps not be surprised to learn that some employers do not always inform candidates that they have been unsuccessful. Sometimes they get so many applications that this is a major administrative effort and they do not bother. Other times, they get a more modest number but are just downright negligent, and this happens with large companies as well as small. If you have gone to all the trouble of applying for a position which they themselves have advertised, you deserve a reply. Phone them and inquire politely how your application is progressing. Try not to be too combative at this stage though, as that could be rather counterproductive.

The personal job record is a good tool. It streamlines and rationalizes the process of responding to advertised positions. In addition to it you need to keep copies of your application forms; the CV you supplied; the original advertisements you replied to; and, ideally, printouts of web information on the company; other company documents such as brochures; and job and/or person specifications supplementary to the form itself.

Part Four

Interviews

CV plus one

Congratulations! Being invited to an interview is a significant achievement. You have got this far because they have seen your CV or application form and your covering letter, and they think you might be the right person for the job. You have beaten your rivals. You have got off the long list and made it to the short list.

If you don't think this is anything to celebrate, and you are filled with a sense of dread at the prospect, consider this: you can now afford to jettison a lot of your fears. When you sent out your CV or application form, you might have worried that you were unqualified for the post, that you were too old or young, or that your transferable skills didn't convince anybody. Now all these fears can be put to one side. Now you need to prove to the interviewer that, of the candidates on the short list, you are the one who is best for the job.

The CV section of this book had a simple message. The CV contains only two types of information: skills and achievements. The interview is a live-action version of the same thing. It is a chance to sell your skills and achievements.

The interview will often take a lead from the CV (or application form). The interviewer will have it on their desk, and if they have not, you should have a copy of it in your briefcase to give to them. The interview will often follow the structure of your CV. At or near the top are your key skills or key achievements, depending on what you see as the stronger. They will be supported by real examples, using real numbers and quantifiable benefits, such as:

> *Set up dedicated in-house database management department, saving an estimated £30,000 in computer consultancy fees per annum.*

When the interviewer sees this, the natural thing to do is to ask further questions, such as:

- How did you arrive at that figure of £30,000?
- Over how many years did you spread the set-up costs?

You must be ready with the answers. The CV or application form is like a shorthand document which you now need to expand for the interviewer's benefit.

The title of this section is 'CV plus one'. The 'one' is you. You are the embodiment of that CV, and much more besides. You are the final reason for success or failure at interview.

This may seem like a lot of emphasis to place on your performance in one nerve-racking half hour, but that is the way it is. All the short-listed candidates, having got to the interview stage, are likely to be at a similar level of ability. The interview is for one thing only: to decide who is the stronger candidate, over and above that high level of ability. The interviewer will be judging you on things which are not available for them in your paper documents: your appearance, your body language, your attitude, your confidence, your defence of your CV, your quick-wittedness, your fluency in answering questions and your perceived trustworthiness. Even such a nebulous quantity as whether or not you 'fit in' to the company in question can be crucial.

The interview, then, showcases the paper you plus the real you, and the way they interact and support each other.

First impressions

We are used to making snap judgements about people. Think of someone that you met for the first time recently. You may have shaken hands and exchanged a few words. In that brief encounter you are likely to have made several judgements about them. You probably felt, after that short meeting, that you could deduce the following:

- What social class they belonged to
- How successful or how wealthy they were
- How much education they had
- Whether or not they could be trusted
- What they thought of you

We are, it seems, programmed to make rapid judgements in social situations. Interviewers are of course aware that people are more than they immediately seem, and that it might take some investigation to find the ideal candidate. They must to some extent override their programming. But, given that, they are social animals like the rest of us. A good first impression still goes a long way.

Think of the impact that a well-dressed, smiling, confident person makes when they walk into a room. To a certain extent, it indicates to the rest of the people in the room what is coming next.

Dress

Some experts will tell you that you should always dress to look your best, but this is not necessarily good advice. If you were applying for work as a gardener, turning up in an immaculate suit for an interview which involved a trip round the grounds would not be appropriate.

That does not mean that in every situation you should dress as you would do if you got the job. In the case above, you should not wear old, worn and dirty clothes and Wellington boots. The best rule is to go 'one up' from the style of dress you would be likely to adopt in the post. That way you will signal that you are attempting to look smart but not look so smart that it seems inappropriate. Here are some examples:

Job	Dress for job	'One up' dress for interview
Nursery care worker	Informal, jeans, cardigan/jumper, sensible shoes/trainers	Skirt or smart trousers and blouse for women; jacket and shirt for men, not necessarily tie
Bank clerk	Suit and tie for men but often in shirt-sleeves; for women, some jewellery, hair may be loose	Trouser or skirt suit for women, hair tied back, no jewellery; smart suit and tie for men

Whatever style of clothing you adopt it should always be neat and well-ironed. Men should remember to keep their ties clean and well-pressed; the knot of the tie is in the region of the face where the gaze tends to be concentrated.

Also remember that interviewers are conservative generally, so don't wear anything too flamboyant.

Colours

As far as colours are concerned, clothing that matches the colours of your eyes, skin and hair is always more likely to look good; a dark colouring with dark hair looks particularly impressive with a dark (navy or dark grey) suit, and light blue eyes and grey/blond hair look good with a charcoal outfit. Red eyes go with a hangover and should be avoided at interview.

Generally speaking, dark colours have more authority, and bright colours have more personality.

Accessories

Try to keep accessories such as jewellery, handbags, briefcases and papers to a minimum. Just one simple folder will often be enough.

As for jewellery, less is more; flashy earrings or bangles act as a distraction from what you are actually saying, and you might be inclined, in your more nervous moments, to play with them.

Hair

Hair, like dress, is a way of signalling that you fit in. Smartly and recently trimmed or styled hair will make a good impression in most cases. However, bear in mind that your hairstyle should, in an ideal world, reflect the type of job you are applying to do. If for example you apply for a job as a rock music journalist and you turn up looking like an accountant, you are more likely to fail the interview.

For all styles of hair a good rule is to make sure it does not get in the way of your eyes. Teenagers often cultivate a long fringe that prevents eye contact, but adopting the same strategy at interview is rather counterproductive. If you have long hair, tie it or comb it neatly back. This says a lot about your openness and professionalism and suggests you have nothing to hide.

Shoes

Many people (men as well as women) say that the first thing they look at to assess a person is their shoes: this is worth heeding. The minimum you need to do in an interview situation is to make sure your shoes are clean and well cared for. Whether they are new and fashionable is likely to be unimportant, unless the job involves some kind of fashion or modelling work.

Socks are probably more important even than shoes. Odd socks could be a severe distraction, and even socks which fail to match the shoe colour or are too vibrant in design could have negative effects.

Hands

Clean your nails after you polish your shoes.

Deodorant and antiperspirant

If you have just had a shower or bath you are likely to be clean enough not to need a deodorant, but you might like to ask someone close enough for their opinion, or if you are really unsure and don't wish to embarrass yourself or anyone else, use one anyway. Interviews are very stressful occasions and if you tend to sweat this will be noticeable, so use an antiperspirant that works.

Body language

The phrase 'body language' involves what are technically known as 'non-verbal cues': things that we do to accompany speech or instead of speech. In an interview situation you will usually be sitting, which limits the non-verbal cues you can exhibit, but you will still be capable of a wide range of them. To be more in control of the interview process it is wise to think about this area to see what signals you are giving, and how you can control them to make a good impression.

Start off by walking confidently into the room where the interview is to take place. If you have been invited to go in by the receptionist, don't knock on the door first. Why? The receptionist has asked you to go in because the interviewer has told them to ask you to go in. Knocking on the door is unnecessary and suggests that you are feeling tentative or nervous.

When walking, try to move freely and naturally: don't shuffle, break into a nervous run, lope or stoop. Swing your arms and walk with a confident stride.

Shake hands with a smile. If there is a panel of people in the room, shake hands all round with smiles, and don't rush it. Let them feel you are happy to be there.

Sit with your hands in your lap or resting lightly on the arms of the chair. Sit up straight, with a very slight forward lean. Don't wring your hands, nervously flex them, crack your knuckles or play with your hair or jewellery, and don't clutch the arms of the chair as if you are awaiting execution.

Legs should be bent and placed in front of the chair, or crossed at the ankles. Do not cross them with one knee on top of the other. That looks as if you are bunching yourself up defensively. You can also bring one leg back under the chair and put one leg slightly forward. That is an easy posture that retains a degree of formality.

When listening to questions, nod occasionally to show you are attending to what the interviewer is saying. When replying, again lean forward slightly. Make your expression appropriate to the words you are saying: say warm, friendly and inviting things with a smile, and grow more serious to answer factual questions.

The most assured interview candidates maintain eye contact for a good portion of the time, but take care also to be deferential and polite. This means that glances 'away', are perfectly permissible and even desirable, to avoid the impression of unwelcome staring. People who look down or away most of the time while they are asking or answering questions though are perceived as nervous, untrustworthy or socially unskilled.

If offered coffee or tea in the interview, it is better to decline it politely. It is possible that you could spill it, which would be disastrous for your composure. Neither should you smoke, even if offered cigarettes. All your energies should be involved in looking professional and answering questions.

Don't be fazed by the telephone ringing during the interview. (Though do make sure it is not yours: remember to switch off your mobile phone before you are called in for interview.) You can read your folder if the interviewer is having a conversation for longer than a minute or so.

Voice

Don't depart from your natural speaking voice. Be relaxed and warm and allow your enthusiasm to shine through but not so much that you begin to squeak or appear worked up. Try not to be too hesitant or breathy, to sigh or use extended 'ums' and 'ahs', although a reasonable use of these will indicate that you are relaxed, since these sorts of vocal signals are a normal part of speech.

Gesture

Some experts recommend powerful gestures such as clutching the air, fondling an imaginary globe, putting one hand out as if holding an imaginary tray, putting hands on hips. The best advice is to keep gestures down to a minimum. There can be a fine line between gesturing and fidgeting, and if we are nervous our nerves will migrate most readily into our gestures, which instead of looking powerful, will look spasmodic, uncontrolled or excessive. A controlled but relaxed posture and mimimal gesturing is more likely to win the day; gestures, like drinking coffee, are liable to carry unacceptable risks.

Being there

Leave home early for the interview in case you get delayed en route. If you get there with twenty minutes to spare, that's no problem. You can use the time to your advantage by observing the staff and visiting the toilets, and if it is a large firm you can have a look round the building, or visit the cafeteria. Don't do last-minute revision for your upcoming interview, though. Even if the interviewer does not come out to greet you, you may be observed by the reception-desk staff, who may later be asked for their opinion of your demeanour by the interviewer.

If you are wearing a heavy coat, take it off, if possible, and find somewhere to hang it before walking into the interview. Sitting steaming in a wet coat while you talk about your unique suitability for the job does not look professional.

Try not to carry a briefcase which is exceptionally large or overstuffed. The smaller, neater and newer your briefcase, the cooler and better prepared you will look. Even just a folder containing your CV is fine. You don't really need anything else by this stage. If you are not prepared by now, you never will be. If you have brought five volumes of the company report with you to read on the train, leave them at the front desk before the interview. The exception to this is if you have brought materials which will form part of the interview, such as samples of work.

As soon as you arrive, even if you have a lot of time to spare, you should consider yourself effectively 'on stage'. A web developer, who was asked for interview, arrived early so decided to spend some time in the cafeteria. Unfortunately he didn't realize that his interviewer was in the cafeteria as well and had watched him argue with a member of the cafeteria staff about the fact that the drinks machine didn't work.

As already mentioned, the front-desk staff may occasionally be asked for input. What impressions did they form of the candidate? Was she/he bright and friendly, or monosyllabic and dour? The opinions of these co-workers might conceivably swing the situation, so be nice to them.

Room layout

As previously mentioned, if you are invited to go into the interview room, go straight in without knocking and shake hands with the interviewer (or interviewers) with a smile. Walk normally across the room with a confident gait.

The interviewer may be behind a desk with your chair in front of it. This is the conventional layout and is now thought to be rather authoritarian, so interviewers often try to change it slightly by having you at the side of the desk; the effect is largely the same. It allows the interviewer to hide behind the desk (remember, they can get nervous too) but it also allows you to hide, since your lower body is not so easily visible. A more 'open' arrangement, in which the interviewer and interviewee face each other sitting down and without an intervening desk, can actually be more uncomfortable.

Sit in the chair provided without asking to sit. That is what it is there for, unless there is a choice of likely chairs. In the latter case say 'May I sit here?' Some books will advise you never to sit on soft furnishings since they are difficult to get up from, but if an armchair is the only chair in the room it would be unwise to insist on remaining on your feet.

The panel interview

Panel interviews are generally thought to be more intimidating than ordinary interviews, but since the bulk of any interview will usually be the fielding of questions by the candidate, you will not be doing anything substantially different to the tasks you would face in a one-to-one interview. Each member of the panel may have a different position in the organization, such as human resources manager, department head or team leader, so they may ask different questions which relate to their position. Again, this does not present any special challenges, since if there were only a single interviewer that person would have to cover all the bases alone.

The truth of the matter though is that there are more of them than there are of you. You need to fight against feeling automatically cowed by this. Try to think of them all as humans with their own fears and insecurities. Have they ever faced unemployment or redundancy? Almost certainly, yes.

Also try not to be aware of them judging you as you walk in: instead, judge them. When you walk in, go up to each member of the panel in turn and shake hands with them, making eye contact with each one and assessing them in your mind. Think about their human foibles and weaknesses.

During a panel interview, don't treat the people there as a group entity and fail to make eye contact with any of them. Again, consider them all as human beings who desire interpersonal contact. When an interviewer from a panel asks a question, you should reply directly to that person, making the occasional glance towards the rest of the panel, and finishing your answer with your eyes on the person who asked the question. If you let your eyes stray to the rest of the panel throughout your answer the questioner may subconsciously feel slighted.

The multiple interview

It is quite possible that an interview, advertised in the singular, might turn out to be an interview in the plural. A common situation is to have an interview with human resources (or personnel) followed by an interview with management. This arrangement may not be announced in advance.

Do not treat the human resources interview as of lesser importance or as a sort of preliminary. You will drastically reduce your chances if you do so. Neither should you panic because you have only prepared for an interview with management. Interviews are interviews. They are all designed to find out whether you are the best person for the job, and as such the questions will essentially be the same. Human resources may be more focused on practical details such as relocation, hours, job-sharing, but you must be prepared to answer these questions anyway, regardless of who is asking them.

Think of the multiple interview as another opportunity to shine. If you do less well than you had hoped in one of the interviews, you can always compensate by turning in a much better performance in the other.

Presentations

Presentations may be used as part of an interview, usually if the job requires you to speak in public or involves a great deal of interpersonal contact or contact with the public.

Presentations will be of three types:

- where you can choose the subject
- where the subject is given to you days beforehand
- where the subject is given to you at the interview

In the first you would be well advised to choose something that relates to the company and its field of operations. Speaking on 'My pet tortoise' for ten minutes is unlikely to impress your potential employer.

In the second type, you have the opportunity to research the topic thoroughly. Specimen presentation subjects might include:

- Ethical sales in the 21st century
- Developing this post over the next five years
- Customer services – what they should mean
- The strengths and weaknesses of the XYZ Corporation
- The opportunities in the XYZ Industry in the next ten years
- How I would prioritize the tasks of this job
- Good staff management

In the third type, you will be told several days or weeks beforehand that a presentation is part of the interview, and that you will only be given the subject of the presentation after arrival. You will then be given some time to prepare it. The secret of success in this type is to prepare as many potential presentations beforehand along the lines of those above: even if you don't hit on exactly the right subject, you will be familiar with the task of putting a presentation together and will be less likely to panic.

In preparing your presentation, go back to something mentioned in the covering letters section: a three-act structure. Take one of the examples given above: 'Ethical sales in the 21st century'.

You could divide it into three parts:

1. What do we mean by ethical sales?
2. Are ethical sales compatible with free market economics?
3. What are the advantages to any particular company of selling ethically?

You can put the three parts, and perhaps some of the ways you have subdivided them, on a handout, which you can then distribute to the audience. Handouts are an excellent way of involving the audience in what you are doing. They also give you a much-needed breather while you hand them round.

You may feel that the object of the exercise is to give the interviewers or staff information on the topic (note that some companies ask you to make the presentation before the staff you may be working with, or even before the other interview applicants). This is the wrong way of looking at it. Ultimately the subject of your presentation is you. You are presenting yourself and your abilities. The material could be anything; it need not be particularly elaborate, technical or complicated, nor need it be new, groundbreaking, amazing or hilarious. If you attempt any of these things you are more likely to flounder. What your presentation should be, in terms of style, is clear, well-thought-out, logical, with a good flow and, if possible, interesting and enthusiastically delivered. That is all that is required.

As the focus will be on you, not the material, stand with a relaxed, comfortable posture. Speak in a voice pitched slightly louder than your usual voice. You may wish to include more expansive gestures than you would use if talking to a colleague close up, since you are addressing an audience, some of whom might be a few metres away, but don't overdo it unless you feel really comfortable. If you use devices such as projectors or flip charts, familiarize yourself with them beforehand so you don't fumble and waste time.

All this takes practice. Don't imagine you can pull a good performance out of the bag without any preparation. Try practising (in your interview clothes) in front of a mirror, or in front of friends. You might be surprised to see how much confidence this gives you when it comes to the real thing.

A final issue is to do with timing. You will be expected to keep to set guidelines for the length of your presentation, typically 5–15 minutes, rarely more or less. Going over or under the set length will incur penalties, and again practice is important. The more the better.

Some pre-interview do's and don'ts

To summarize, here are checklists of the do's and don'ts so far:

Do

- Wear clean, well-pressed clothing and clean, well-kept shoes
- Remember that you are a success for getting on to the short list
- Wear colours that are appropriate for your eyes and skin colouring, and for the job
- Arrive early
- Leave your overcoat and any bulky items at the desk
- Establish friendly relations with all staff you meet
- Shake hands with everyone present in the interview room
- Remember the interviewers are human
- Nod to show you are attending to what they are saying
- Make eye contact
- Practise presentations

Don't

- Smoke
- Drink coffee or alcohol
- Wear too much jewellery
- Wear your hair over your face
- Dress inappropriately to the organization or position
- Sit with your knees crossed 'high'
- Fidget
- Make large gestures with your hands or arms
- Do conspicuous last-minute cribbing in the reception area
- Knock on the door as you go into the interview room
- Favour one method of making an impression (for example dress) over others, such as what you are actually going to say

Mental preparation

Nerves

Nerves do not show as much as you think. You may feel that your heart is pounding, your mouth is dry, and your head is swimming, but none of these is actually visible. Concentrate on the fact that however you are feeling, outwardly you appear normal. It may help you to calm down.

A high level of nervous anticipation is to be expected. Everyone gets nervous. Accept your nerves and take them as part of your performance. Recognizing that your nerves are normal will also help calm you down.

If neither of these is working, take deep breaths before you go into the interview room. A good supply of blood oxygen makes you less likely to start hyperventilating or feel short of breath in the opening stages.

Some people adopt exaggerated behaviour when they get nervous. They may gesture wildly, adopt exaggeratedly relaxed poses, or play with things. If you notice you have a propensity to this, gently curb it, bringing your body back to a more neutral pose. This is not the moment for experimentation in posture or gesture.

Use the 'worst that can happen' rule. If you don't put in a good performance, you may not get the job. But how much does that really matter? You are on the road to success, even if you don't achieve it this time. You have made it to the short list after all. If you keep trying and keep making short lists, sooner or later you will get the job you want. It is inevitable. And if you don't get this particular job, the process will be a valuable learning experience.

Focus on the idea that despite your anxieties you are going to do the best job you can.

Positive Mental Movie

It may help if you employ some techniques for positive visualization before your interview. There are many of these but here is one of the most popular. It is called the 'Positive Mental Movie'.

To use this method, take some time to think about what you want in your life, both in the personal and working spheres. Write the areas in which you would like to see change on the left-hand side of a piece of paper, and on the right-hand side write how you intend to make these changes. For example:

Aim	Method of achieving aim
Move house	Get your house ready for sale; explore property market
Find more satisfying work	Go to careers advice centre
Earn more money	Consider reskilling

Visualize a day at some point in your future when you have achieved these changes, and visualize what such a day would be like in its actual details. Where would you be when you woke up? What would you do in the morning? What sort of work would you do or go to? What sort of people would you meet? How would you behave towards them? You can run it as a film inside your mind.

The difference between this and an unfocused dream of happiness is that each item is 'costed'. You have thought not only about what you want, but how you are going to get it.

Now take the job you are going for and insert it as part of your mental movie. See yourself as part of the organization you are applying to work with, and the job as part of your new life. It does not matter if, on this occasion, you don't get this particular post. If it does not come now, something similar will soon, as long as you work towards it.

So far we have looked at dress, posture, gesture, grooming, accessories, non-verbal cues, voice, pre-interview behaviour, likely interview set-up, presentations and mental preparation. Now we have to consider the actual questions.

As mentioned previously, the interview is your 'CV plus one'. It is a chance to present your skills and achievements through the lens of your personality. Having covered the best way to appear, speak and think, let's look at what you should actually say.

Five rules for answering questions

1. Answer in terms of your skills and achievements.

If the question is 'What do you think you could bring to this post?', you have been given a gift. Talk about your capabilities (taking a lead from the profile section on your CV), the areas in which you have had an impact at work, your technical proficiencies and strengths, the money or time you have saved or the income you have generated. Other questions which lead naturally on to your skills and achievements are: 'What was the most important thing you learned in your last job?', 'Are you a good manager?' and 'Why should we employ you?'

Other questions may not seem so promising. Even so, do still try to answer in terms of your skills and achievements. For example, if they say 'You don't seem to have much experience in the XY sector', begin: 'That's true, but ...' and weigh in with your transferable skills and the past achievements that make you a great prospect for the post. They know from your CV that you don't have much experience in the XY sector, but they still put you on the short list; now is your chance to confirm that they made the right decision.

Another question might be: 'Have you ever had any difficulties with staff?' This can easily be turned around to benefit you. The answer could be 'No, I don't think so. I have always had good relations with my co-workers and with members of the team who worked for me. At XZ Corporation I worked as section leader of a team of twenty, and they always knew they could bring their problems to me. We had an open-plan office and it was very friendly and informal ...' etc. There is no benefit in giving negative information (see point 4).

2. Don't always answer only the question.

Questions are opportunities to present your skills and achievements, not just requests for factual information. Always take the opportunity to expand on your answer and show what distinguishes you from other candidates and why you are the best for the job.

So, the message is, answer the question, certainly – employers don't like candidates who ignore the question – but use it to lead on to what you want to tell them.

3. Agree with the interviewer, don't confront them.

Imagine a situation in which the interviewer looks at your CV and says: 'I see there is quite a big gap here.' Don't respond by saying: 'No, that's not true, look down there at the bottom there, I did voluntary work.' You may well be technically correct, but it is not going to win you a friend. It would be better to say 'Yes, that's quite true. I took time out to work on a cocoa plantation in Costa Rica. I learned a lot from that. That was a wonderful year for me ...' etc.

Although the information content is essentially the same, the two responses are quite different in tone.

4. Be positive, not negative.

You should certainly never volunteer negative information. Some interviewees will do this out of a desire to appear truthful, frank and self-aware, but it is a mistake. You are in a competitive situation. If, in reply to an open question about your abilities you say something like 'I can sometimes be a bit grumpy in the mornings', even as a joke, you will be marked down. Negative information makes employers nervous and they tend to enquire further, which means that if you have volunteered any you will then be invited to dig yourself deeper into your hole.

It is different if you are asked to give negative information. Such questions will come in the form 'What are your weaknesses?' or 'Tell me about something that you have found difficult at work.'

Employers like to ask you to give negative information to see what sort of person you are. If you can project yourself as someone who sees problems as opportunities you will seem much more employable. Questions about weaknesses or faults therefore are a chance to put a positive spin on an essentially negative situation. In the second example above they are asking you to describe a problem. Take these three principles as guidelines:

- make it something that happened a long time ago
- show that you learned from it
- demonstrate that you then surmounted similar problems afterwards

This will allow you to take the failure or weakness they are asking for and magically turn it into something that makes you sound like an attractive prospect.

5. Give them what they want.

When answering questions you should try to say what employers want to hear. The certainty is that all the candidates want the post for the benefits of promotion, increased salary, and personal development that it will bring them. To mention these would be superfluous. It is more beneficial to tell the employer what is in it for them.

To prepare for this, do some brainstorming on the job advertisement, using the methods in the 'Covering statement' section in Part Two (page 79):

- Study the job specification and person specification. Take each point and write notes to match it. Do not omit any.
- Use transferable skills and voluntary work to cover all the elements if you are missing something.
- Think about the personality of the person they are looking for, and try to project yourself as that person.
- Research the company and get to know its objectives and philosophy.

It is also a good idea to plan how you will respond if you are asked something that you cannot answer at the interview. If you prepare a ready-made form of words for such a situation then you can have recourse to it in emergencies. It could be something like: 'Ah, I have never been asked that before. I'd like to think about that to give you a considered answer, because I think it is an interesting question … Can we come back to it?' In the course of saying that, you might have thought of something anyway.

Common questions

The questions below are some of the most common ones you will encounter. Use the suggestions underneath each question, then think through your own answer. When you have a good idea of what your response is going to be, practise talking through your answer out loud, as if you were replying to the interviewer. This is invaluable preparation: actually speaking, and merely thinking about speaking, are two radically different activities.

Perhaps this is also the place to emphasize that although you are going to be doing a good deal of selective presentation of your skills and achievements, you should never tell lies.

'What do you see as your strengths?'

You will have plenty of leads in your CV for your strengths. Try, however, to match your strengths to the particular organization you are dealing with. Another thing to be aware of here is that you are being asked to tell the interviewer in no uncertain terms what your good points are. This is the moment for plain, direct speaking about what you could offer. Don't use tentative language such as 'I feel' or 'rather'. Consider the following:

✘ *I feel I'm quite motivated ...*

✘ *I think I'm quite good at getting on with people ...*

Now consider the greater impact of the following:

✔ *I'm very motivated: I feel a sense of personal involvement in this field because ...*

✔ *I enjoy working with people ...*

As a variant on this try presenting your skills and achievements as 'endorsements' from others:

✔ *My friends are always telling me I'm very persistent ...*

Endorsements avoid those destructive qualifiers and sound a bit more modest if that is what you think the situation calls for. They bring in a third-party opinion as an objective arbiter.

'What are your reasons for applying for this post?'

As mentioned above, do not couch your answer in terms of what you are hoping to gain by applying for the post, even though the question seems to be inviting you to do just that. Instead, talk in terms of the contribution you believe you could make. Draw attention to the skills that you have, talk about how you share the company's goals, say how you find the company's work exciting (enthusiastic candidates are often more successful), mention how your recent experience makes you particularly qualified for this job, and emphasize how much you enjoy leading and motivating others (where appropriate).

Don't be afraid to repeat and elaborate on material that is in your CV. Each snippet of information on your CV, each skill and achievement, should be capable of elaboration, and it is wise to practise elaborating these beforehand.

'What did you learn from your last job?'

Tell stories.

Stories are the most powerful way of answering questions like this because they can show what you learned in a memorable, dramatic form. People listening to a story understand that this is a structured set-piece intended to entertain and, in this case, make a point.

Which stories should you tell? Why, stories of your successes, of course. Think of an occasion where you came across something at work that you did not initially understand or know how to deal with, how you grappled with it and how you became familiar with it and mastered it:

> *When I was doing temporary work in my summer break during the final year of my degree I worked in a coleslaw-packing factory. It involved working on a production line*

> *where the coleslaw was dispensed into little pots on a conveyor belt. On one occasion the machine malfunctioned. The part dispensing the pots jammed, and the machine started throwing coleslaw everywhere. I was surprised to see everyone just looking at it without moving. I got off my seat and went round to the rear of the machine where there was an 'off' switch and shut the machine down. After that I noticed people started treating me differently. I realized that if you take the initiative people's attitude changes towards you.*

Stories have a plot: a set-up, action and a pay-off. The pay-off is what you learned and how you applied it afterwards. Unless you have rehearsed the story beforehand it is unlikely it will come across with the right pace and punch, and you will not make the point that the story was designed for. The more you practise this the more fluent you will become.

'How would you describe yourself?'

Look at the profile section on your CV, though try not to simply repeat it word for word. You need to communicate the idea that you have a background of demonstrable achievement and the skills to make a valuable contribution to the new company. For example:

> *I am an active person, I spend most of my waking time doing things, I am rarely bored and I take a creative attitude to life in general. I work well in high-pressure situations and I like to deal with complex problems. I'm proud of the way I took forward the modernization of my post at XZ Inc. At work I'm very target-driven and I enjoy the challenge of motivating staff. I like to think of myself as a good communicator.*

HOW TO ANSWER QUESTIONS

'What are your reasons for leaving your present position?'

Of course, you may never be asked this, because you may not be going straight from one job to another. But if you are still in work, you are in a rather strange situation psychologically: the potential employer (ie the interviewer) feels more of a sense of kinship with your present employer than he does with you. That is only to be expected. Like your present employer, your interviewer is concerned about your loyalty, your reliability and your trustworthiness. If they see that you are leaving casually, for selfish reasons, without giving a thought to your current boss and his staff problems, they are less likely to see you as an attractive option.

How do you get around this ticklish situation? Well, the first thing to bear in mind is that all employers need staff, and the possibility that staff might leave is a risk that has to be taken. Staff turnover can run as high as 40% per annum in some large organizations.

The second thing to be borne in mind is that you can still present your reasons for leaving or wanting to leave in the best light possible. Have a look on page 77 in Part Two for a table showing some common reasons for leaving and the ways you can present them.

The third thing to be borne in mind is that, whatever reason you give, you should always present your relationship with a previous employer as being one of complete cordiality. Never imply any criticism of them. This will only give the impression that you are a potential source of trouble.

'Have you been doing anything since you left your last job?'

A veiled way of talking about unemployment. The question could also refer to CV gaps; what you were doing in the period between episodes of obvious work. You must have an answer ready, since this is an area that all employers will be interested in and concerned about. Unemployment need not be unproductive. It can even be turned in your favour.

Voluntary work can be an opportunity to talk about the acquisition of valuable new skills and show your concern for your community. If you have taken time out for a pregnancy or for child care this is perfectly legitimate. You can give details of foreign travel or service overseas. All of these give you the opportunity to show the acquisition of new skills and achievements.

'Can you give us an example of how you dealt with a difficult situation at work?'

This is another example of a 'gift' question, as long as you prepare for it well. The idea here is to talk about a problem, explain why it was a problem, show how you solved it, and then show how you were able to deal with or prevent similar problems subsequently. An example might be a late delivery that angered a lot of customers. You can show how by staying calm, delegating responsibility or thinking creatively you solved the problem and put procedures in place to forestall similar problems in future.

If you can talk about a problem-solving capability that is useful in the job you are applying for, such as knowledge of first aid in a job that involved care for the elderly or vulnerable, this will add to the relevance and impressiveness of the achievement.

'What are your personal faults?'

Again, the employer is asking you to give negative information. Some career books will advise you at this point to give an answer that is pitched like a weakness, but is actually a strength, such as: 'I work too hard' or 'I show too much commitment to my job'. However, this is a rather transparent strategy. A better way of dealing with it is to admit to a real weakness, but make it a very minor one. For example you could say: 'Sometimes I can be very stubborn, although I'm aware of that now and try not to push things too hard when I don't get my way.' This minor fault is qualified by 'sometimes', which makes it pretty forgiveable. More importantly, stubbornness is the flip-side of persistence, and someone who is stubborn is likely to be persistent, and vice versa. You will also notice that the reply makes this fault a past fault. The interviewer has asked you for a fault but you have given him/her one that no longer exists.

Another example is to mention a minor fault that has no bearing on the job you are applying for. For example, 'I'm sometimes a bit clumsy. I seem to break plates a lot.' If you are applying for work in a post that does not require you to be particularly dextrous, then this is an example of a fault with little or no downside.

'Would you say you are an ambitious person?'

This is an opportunity to talk about your career plans and to roll out your 'career objective' (see page 26). However, make sure you include your prospective employer in them. If your plans involve moving on to a different organization or a different job entirely, then keep quiet about them. Try instead to show how you are looking forward to developing a long relationship with the person who is interviewing you. Recruiting is an expensive business so if you plan to leave after a few months you will be a waste of their time and money.

'Do you think it is important for people to have equal opportunities at work, and can you say why?'

Of course it will be important, but the sting in the tail is to say why. If you have personal experience, talk about that, since that will always have the greatest impact. If you don't have any personal stories to tell, talk about friends' experiences.

You can talk about a number of different areas here. Equal opportunities cover issues of sex, race, sexuality, age, marital status, culture, nationality, religion, disability or HIV status. You are more likely to have to field this question in jobs where there is some kind of community relations or health content. Remember that the reason the employer wants to talk about this is because it is an important part of their brief to comply with current equal opportunity legislation and to recruit people who are aware of equal opportunity legislation. If you can make it clear in your answer that you are aware not only of the ethical side of this but also the legal side, you will make a much better impression. Legislation to look at, available to view online as well as in public libraries, includes the Race Relations Act, the Sex Discrimination Act, the Employment Equality (Sexual Orientation) Act, the Equal Pay Act and the Disability Discrimination Act.

'What are your interests outside work?'

Interviewers ask about interests because they believe they can be very revealing. What people do in their spare time is 'transferable'. Someone who enjoys paragliding is different from someone who flies kites.

Sports say a lot about you. Have a look again at some of the categories mentioned in Part One:

- Team sports (football, netball etc): good interpersonal skills, ability to delegate and/or lead
- Individual competitive sports (cycling, climbing, etc): determination, aggression, self-motivation
- Cerebral sports (chess, bridge, etc): intelligence, curiosity, analytical skills

If you have ever been appointed to a position, such as the leader of a club, or president of a society, say so.

Something unusual to talk about might enliven what can be a humdrum experience for an interviewer, and they may decide to ask several follow-up questions out of sheer curiosity. An interview like this could cement your candidacy in the mind of the interviewers.

It would probably be a mistake, however, if the discussion goes on too long, because in a competitive situation you must make mention of your essential skills and achievements. Interview time is limited.

'What do you think you could contribute to this post particularly?'

This is similar to 'What are your reasons for applying for this post?', only framed in such a way that you are asked explicitly to talk about your contribution. So, as above, talk about your skills and achievements, how you share the company's goals, how you find the company's work exciting, how much you enjoy leading and motivating others.

Another way of looking at this question is to note the emphasis on 'particularly'. You have a chance here to set yourself against other candidates. Two things will be of relevance: firstly the parts of your CV that come closest to the activities and ethos of the particular company, and secondly the personal qualities that make you 'fit in' to that particular company. As already mentioned, employers will sometimes take a candidate who 'fits in' over another candidate with more obvious qualifications. Do as much research as you can to find out what sort of person they want for the job.

'Do you know much about this company?'

A common question and a good chance to make an impression. The more research you can do the better. If you can lead off with a remark such as 'I saw an interesting article recently in *New Business* magazine ...' that will give you something concrete to discuss.

'What sort of people do you get on best with?'

A good opportunity to lead into an example of your interpersonal skills. Again, start by answering the question, then go further: 'I get on well with most people … when I was at XY company I led a small team of four …' etc.

'Do you have any questions for us?'

This is an opportunity, but not necessarily an opportunity to ask a question! If you feel that you have no questions to ask (which is fine) then say something like: 'I don't think so at the moment, but may I contact you if I think of anything else?' This gives the impression that you are really keen and don't want to just rush out of the office.

You can also use this question as a way of confirming your interest in the post. Something like: 'No, but I'd just like to say thank you for the opportunity to meet you like this and I would be very interested in taking the job if it was offered.'

Another useful strategy is to say: 'I don't have a question as such, but could I mention one thing that I think is particularly relevant about my skills and experience?' (pause for confirmation). If they say 'certainly' at this point, they have then given you carte blanche to get in anything that you don't think has been covered so far, and the chance to underline your essential rightness for the post. Make it brief, concise and to the point. Then finish off by thanking them again.

This is not the point to ask about salary. Look into that when you get the offer (see below).

If you really have no questions and don't need to say anything beyond thanking them politely and expressing your continuing interest, don't make up questions for the sake of it. They may sound false, or worse, may concern something that you should know the answer to or even something that has already been mentioned.

Pay negotiation

Only negotiate after you have been offered the job. If you start getting tough on pay when you are still just one candidate among many, you have just handed them a reason to pass you over. On the other hand, if they have offered you the post, they are unlikely to go back on their offer to you because you are beginning to negotiate. It would mean going into reverse on the selection procedure, and possibly even re-interviewing.

You will probably have some idea of the pay before you go for the interview, especially if it was an advertised position. It might be in a band between two figures, or it might be an approximate figure. You will thus be able to gauge whether this represents a potential raise or a cut in salary.

If it is a cut in salary, this may or may not be a bad thing. After all, there is more to life than money. Job satisfaction, such as rewarding and enjoyable work, work with lots of holidays, part-time work that lets you spend time with your family, can be much more important than money. Even leaving job satisfaction aside, there are other reasons, from a career point of view, why you might wish to take a cut in pay. You may wish to get a foot in the door of a prestigious organization, for instance. You may wish to get better prospects for promotion. You can always ask for more once you are ensconced and you have proved that you are indispensable.

But if money is important and you need to negotiate a good package to make your move from your present job worthwhile, here are some negotiating rules:

1. Make sure, first of all, that you are talking to the person who has the authority to make a decision.

2. If they have not already done so, ask them to suggest a figure. Don't suggest one yourself, since if you do that you cannot negotiate up, only down!

3. If they ask you to suggest something in return at this point, tell them what your research has told you is a fair price for the post. That is something approaching a third-party opinion, even though it functions effectively as your bid for the post. If you have to back down from it, it will not seem such a personal defeat. Alternatively, say what your current salary is and say you would like to improve on it.

4. If, however, your initial strategy has been successful, and they have been the one to suggest the first figure, it may well be rather on the low side, since their job is to get the best deal possible for the company. If you want then to negotiate this up, don't mention a figure but instead try an open-ended question or statement without a number in it. That way you are not tied to any particular amount, and backing down (if you have to) will not lose you face. Remember that at this stage recruiters are usually prepared to go up. Only they know how much by: that is why you leave the rise to them rather than suggesting it yourself. Ways to get them to state this additional increment include the following:

   - I'm currently earning around that figure and I was hoping to improve on it.
   - That's a little under what I need to move from ZZ Inc. I'm very interested in the post, but would there be any flexibility on that?
   - If you can supply a car I would consider that offer.
   - I would agree to that but I think it is a little below the market

rate. Could I suggest a review in pay some time in the second half of the year?

5. If they then don't suggest an improvement to their previous position, and you want the job, the game is essentially over. If, on the other hand, they don't improve on their position, and that is a serious problem for you (ie you no longer want or can afford to take the job), you have nothing to lose and you can hold out for a higher figure.

Finishing up

Last impressions

First impressions count. So do last impressions. If you get to the point in the interview where you have fielded the 'any other questions' question, the interview is essentially over. A good way of ending the interview is not to do so passively, but to actively leave. You can do this by making a point of thanking the interviewer (if you have not already done so), then reiterating that you are interested in the job:

> I want to thank you for inviting me; it has been very nice to meet you. I was particularly interested to hear about the XYZ development. May I say just before I leave that I am interested in the position because …

Make it brief and courteous.

If it has not already been indicated, it is possible to ask: 'May I ask when you are likely to be making a decision?' This shows you are organized enough to care about what is going to happen next and not just relieved that the interview is over. But too much questioning at this stage can be counterproductive. Don't ask, for instance:

- How did I do?
- Will there be a medical?
- Will there be another interview?

If the interviewer does not want to volunteer any more information at this point, it is best not to press for it. Any more questions are likely to be something of an irritant, since the interviewer has a busy day and needs to go on to the next candidate. The end of the interview should be brief and impressive.

Debrief

After the interview you may wish to take stock of the situation and review your performance. This can be helpful, especially if, on this occasion, you don't get the job. Among the questions worth asking yourself are:

- What were the questions? (write them down for future reference)
- Was I expecting them?
- Did I feel I projected myself well in terms of dress/appearance/body language?
- Do I need more practice in presentations/closing the interview positively/pay negotiation?
- Did I manage to put across my key skills and achievements?
- Did I volunteer, or was I forced into divulging, any negative information?
- Generally, what could I improve?

A further category of questions relates to the implications of actually being offered the job:

- Do I want this job, now I have had a chance to see inside the organization?
- What would relocation mean to me?
- What about the hours/facilities/fringe benefits?
- Does this company have a future?
- Now I have met my boss, would I be able to get on with her/him?
- Would I be able to afford to move? (check the house prices in the area)
- Is the pay fair?

Just because you are offered a job does not mean you have to take it. Remember, you are a valuable commodity.

Telephone and video interviews

By telephone

It has been accepted practice for some time to interview candidates by telephone, especially as a first-round procedure. The main imperative here is cost for the employer. They feel that they can get some idea of the candidate by asking a series of questions similar to the common ones above and filtering candidates before moving them on to face-to-face interviews, or video interviews. It is true that a lot can be gauged from the voice alone. Confidence in answering questions, readiness with the right information, the ability to deal with CV gaps, knowledge of the company, and all of the other things dealt with above, can be gauged pretty effectively just by listening to a person speaking.

This may be less nerve-racking for the candidate too. They may feel more in control of the process if they are on home ground. It is also cheaper for the candidate, although if there is a second stage, the usual costs will apply.

You may only be aware that you are going to be interviewed by phone when the company calls you. It is highly unlikely they will insist on it there and then, however; the normal procedure is to offer the option of having the interview straight away or later at the candidate's convenience. There is no stigma attached to asking to have it later. Most people have busy working lives. It would be unreasonable to expect a phone call at random to find them with a 15-minute space with no distractions.

Suggest a time when you are likely to have no interruptions, when the children are not around and when you are comfortable

that you have done the preparation you need to sell yourself effectively.

By video

Interviews are expensive. They involve costs both for the interviewers, who have to set aside resources for the necessary staffing
hours, paperwork and travel expense claims, and for the candidates, who have to travel to meet the employers. A cheaper alternative is to use video technology to create a virtual interview.

Video interviews are common in sectors in which there are plenty
of vacancies but no trained staff, so that employers need to go further afield, perhaps abroad, to find the right candidates. Interviews
by video are often used to recruit for more senior positions. It is
common, for example, for universities in the UK to hold video interviews with candidates in Sydney or San Francisco for lectureship
positions, and for universities in Australia or the USA to return the
compliment. Again, this might be a first-round process, so candidates should be prepared to have a video interview followed by
a face-to-face meeting.

Video interviews will be of two main types. The first is when the
candidate is filmed being interviewed in a normal setting in the
office of a recruitment consultant. The consultant may interview
the candidate in person or use interviewing software to ask and
record questions. The videotape or disc is then sent to the employer to view. If enough points are scored when the employer sees
the recording, the candidate will either get the job or be invited to
the next stage, which will involve a face-to-face meeting.

In the second, the candidate is interviewed live on camera. This
could be at a recruitment agency or a local company headquarters,
or in the candidate's own home. In the latter case, interviewees
will need a camera and the appropriate software, such as
NetMeeting. The technical requirements here can be a little daunt-

ing for those not familiar with the most modern technology, but the recruiter should help with any technical difficulties. As long as the computer being used is fairly modern, there should be few problems. Here is a checklist of the essential kit:

- A processor with a speed of over 90 MHz (megahertz)
- Over 24 MB (megabytes) of RAM
- An internet connection
- A modem of 56KB/s (kilobytes per second) or higher
- 4MB (megabytes) of free disk space
- A sound card with microphone and speakers
- A video capture card
- A small camera of the type that will sit above your computer

The rules are the same as for real-world interviews:

- Dress smartly
- Get a haircut
- Speak in a voice that is clear and strong
- Smile
- Follow the rules for presenting your skills and achievements
- Rehearse the common questions

There are a couple of things you should be aware of when being videoed as opposed to interviewed by a person who is present in the room.

First of all, keep still. If you move too much from side to side you will move out of shot. Secondly, speak in a voice which is slightly slower and more precise than your usual speaking voice. A stronger, clearer voice will come across better in the video and will enable interviewers to take notes more easily. Thirdly, be aware that there might be a short time lag between giving and receiving answers, both from their side and yours. This might make interruptions more likely if you are not used to it.

Lastly, if the interview is taking place via video link in your own home, make sure the environment you are displaying to the recruiter is presentable. Remove ashtrays, empty cans, children, pets, friends and partners. A suitable environment is an uncluttered, book-lined study; an even better environment is a blank wall.

All interviews, whether by phone, video or in actuality, are about the way your presence as a person supports and enhances your presence on paper. They are your chance to shine and be the centre of attention. Remember that you are being given this chance because you deserve it. Good luck!

Index

INDEX